MW00947116

Frost
Flowers

Thoughts and Observations from the Heartland

JOHN B. DELAP

ARCHWAY
PUBLISHING

This book is a work of non-fiction. Unless otherwise noted, the author
and the publisher make no explicit guarantees as to the accuracy of
the information contained in this book and in some cases, names
of people and places have been altered to protect their privacy.

Archway Publishing books may be ordered
through booksellers or by contacting:

Archway Publishing
1663 Liberty Drive
Bloomington, IN 47403
www.archwaypublishing.com
1 (888) 242-5904

Because of the dynamic nature of the Internet, any web addresses or
links contained in this book may have changed since publication and
may no longer be valid. The views expressed in this work are solely those
of the author and do not necessarily reflect the views of the publisher,
and the publisher hereby disclaims any responsibility for them.

Unless otherwise noted all images were taken by the author.

ISBN: 978-1-4808-7806-8 (sc)
ISBN: 978-1-4808-7804-4 (hc)
ISBN: 978-1-4808-7805-1 (e)

Library of Congress Control Number: 2019907120

Print information available on the last page.

Archway Publishing rev. date: 07/18/2019

Dedication

For my wife, Tracy. Thanks for putting up with me all these years and believing in me.

For my children - Charlie, Sam, Katie, and Sarah. Each hug and "I love you" is so powerful.

Finally, this book is dedicated to the memory of my late parents. You let a young boy start to wander all those years ago and I'm still "lost" in the woods.

Of all the paths you take in life, make sure a few of them are dirt.

- John Muir

and,

We shall not cease from exploration
And the end of all our exploring
Will be to arrive where we started
And know the place for the first time.

- from Little Gidding by T.S. Eliot

and

...there's another world beyond the world of men.

- from *Conversation in the Mountains* by Li Pai

Contents

III. Sanctum Sanctorum

IV. Flora and Fauna

Foreword

"If you talk to yourself and listen, you might find out who you really are." So says my friend, John—"a Hoosier and self-described nature nut." Ah, but there is more to this story than that! That story unfolds with each turn of the page in the book you are holding. I've been privileged to walk along with John on many a Friday morning hike, often through Brown County State Park in south-central Indiana, but other places as well. But when we can't hike together, through the observations and reflections offered herein, I still get to accompany John on these walks through nature, which are, more deeply, a walk through life. There is vulnerability in sharing yourself - how you think, what you feel, how you perceive the world and your place in it - but in allowing us a glimpse into his life, John invites the rest of us to see into our own, that we are not separate from the rest of the bugs and bees and fungi; we are integral parts of forests and mountains and rivers. Such insight recalls us to the deepest roots of our humanity that have been suppressed and left untended by the pace and technology and values of modern society. Enticed by the primordial longing to listen with reverence, we come to realize that how we treat the natural world is how we treat ourselves.

Those of us whose sensibilities are nurtured by the

embrace of our ancient Mother come to know ourselves more deeply in the wonder evoked in the delicate frost flower, in the wonderful balm of the music of the woods, in pondering our own life in the falling leaf that is caught before it rests upon its place of transition to new life birthed from its demise. Listening to the silence, sometimes you just have to let the experience speak its wordless wisdom. Admiring the industriousness of the pileated woodpecker jackhammering its way to its next meal; marveling at the other-worldly echoes of ice quakes; quieting your own noisy steps on the frozen detritus of the forest floor so you can hear the nearly imperceptible tick-tick of tiny snowflakes landing on frosted leaves; stopping to notice the subtle transitions of bud and color at season's change, gladdened by the dancing rhythm and melody of the water babbling over the ledge where you stop to fix tea.... There is much to this story and the story continues to unfold—with each step on the trail, with each moment we are aware that we are part of, not separate from, the natural world, with each turn of the page. Whether contemplating the musings of Thoreau or finding God in more than just a church pew, in accompanying John on these walks through nature, or more deeply, a walk through life, we discover that this is the story, not only of the heart of one from the heartland, this Hoosier and self-described nature nut, but of ourselves—who we really are. So turn the page and step into this story of life, for when it's time to raise a wee nip at the end of the trail "it will have been a damn good walk, but until then..."

- Marc Vance

Preface

One summer long ago, a young barefoot boy bounded out the backdoor of his house, looked at the world around him in wonder and, years later, he has yet to come back inside. I am that boy, still walking in the world, in awe of nature and the life that surrounds me.

It's been over forty years since Mr. Barton, my high school guidance counselor, told me to give up on any plans I had of going to college. I was an indifferent student whose rank was in the bottom half of my class and whose SAT scores were in the toilet. I remember going home and telling my parents, despite Mr. Barton's advice, that I wanted to be a forest ranger. The battery of career tests I had taken suggested I had a lot in common with those in forestry. Dad shot that down as quickly as one would shoot a fox in a hen house. He was of the post-war generation who believed that success was more about the money one made, rather than being happy while making it. At the time, I recall being disappointed but not devastated.

After graduation, I spent one depressing semester at Purdue University—winter of '78 to be exact. The blizzard that hit Indiana that winter was epic, and West Lafayette was no place to be during a snowstorm, trust me. I returned home with little or no idea of what to do with my life. I worked at a box plant, a lumber yard, as a surveyor's assistant, a handyman, an EPA research assistant, a bartender, a laboratory technician, a waiter, and a busboy. I pursued degrees in heating and air conditioning technology, surveying, civil engineering, and business. I wandered aimlessly before a concussion from a bike spill forced me to suspend my quest for an engineering degree. I ended up at Indiana University, where I received my B.A. in political science in 1986 and, at the same time, discovered that I enjoyed writing.

I had buried those dreams of working in the outdoors and done what dutiful sons were supposed to do. I went to work, raised a family, and climbed the ladder. I didn't do too badly: comfortable salary, nice house, two sons, new cars, summer vacations—and then, a divorce. Following the end of my marriage, I began to slowly pick up the pieces. I had never lost my love of the outdoors. Nature was my solace, and now I had more time to spend with my lover.

Five years passed before I remarried, but I never stepped off the ladder—bigger house, better cars, more stuff. Then, about two years ago, I finally fell. I'm not sure what rung I was on. I picked myself up, looked for broken bones, shook off the dust, and put away the ladder. Life is a series of steps and missteps along an uneven and sometimes difficult trail.

Dreams sometimes take a little time to come true. The most recent stop on the trail has afforded me a grand prospect: a wonderful wife, two more children who remind me to live as a child, a modest home, a used truck, a backyard garden, walks in the woods...and my writing.

Back in 2003, twenty-seven years after I took those career interest tests in high school, I decided to take them again. I was in the midst of a possible career change and wanted some guidance. The results were hardly shocking: I was utterly not cut out for my current career in human resources. I had more in common with those in the natural history fields, and a strong correlation to those who write about nature. "What would I write about?" I asked myself. After briefly pondering the question, I did the only thing I could do: I stayed in HR for another fifteen years.

I have always loved field guides. I have well over two hundred on my bookshelves. Six years ago, I stared at them, asking myself if I were ever going to do anything with all that information. That moment was my *Eureka!* and "Upon Common Ground" was born. My boyhood dream of being a forest ranger, my love of nature, and my love of writing all came together in liberating synergy.

My first effort was a periodical newsletter, "Upon Common Ground", but being somewhat dysfunctional at desktop publishing, that project slipped away. After losing my job, I suddenly had a lot of time on my hands. Thus began my blog, and now my first book, however modest the endeavor. Within these pages you will find a potpourri of thoughts, ruminations, pontifications, and opinions on life and the natural world. I continue to mature as a writer, but I believe it's about the journey, not the destination. These are just a few of my observations so far. I hope they find a home with you.

Author's Note

Until three years ago, I hadn't even heard of a frost flower, let alone seen one in person. When I first saw them in the woods of Brown County State Park on a cold winter morning, I was puzzled. But with an assist from the National Weather Service, I discovered the identity of these beautiful white ribbons of ice, and realized just how lucky I was to have seen them that day. Fortunately, I have seen them every year since and never tire of their unique patterns and shapes, each as varied as a snowflake. Frost flowers are quite ephemeral and I count it a blessing to have experienced their beauty.

The weather phenomenon that creates frost flowers is best explained in this short piece by Glen Conner, State Climatologist Emeritus for Kentucky and found at https://www.weather.gov/lmk/frost_flowers –

"Frost flowers are thin layers (perhaps credit card thickness) of ice that are extruded through slits from the stems of white or yellow wingstem plants, among others. Their formation requires freezing air temperature, soil that is moist or wet but not frozen, and a plant's stem that has not been previously frozen. (Practically speaking, a once per year event, although not all individuals produce frost flowers on the first day of good conditions). The water in the plant's stem is drawn upward by capillary action from the ground. It expands as it freezes and splits the stem vertically and freezes on contact with the air. As more water is drawn from ground through the split, it extrudes a paper thin ice layer further from the stem. The length of the split determines if the frost flower is a narrow or wide ribbon of ice. It curls unpredictably as it is extruded, perhaps from unequal friction along the sides of the split, to form 'petals'. These flowers, no two of which are alike, are fragile and last only until they sublimate or melt."

Incidentally, the frost flowers I have seen grow from snakeroot, a common wildflower in Indiana woodlands. I hope you enjoy my frost flowers—short vignettes that will hopefully leave an impression.

I. WAYPOINTS

The Attic of Our Attitudes

This past weekend, I had a text exchange with my sister about a pair of boots. The boots in question belonged to my nephew, and I guess he really didn't like them all that much. Alice was doing a closet purge and wondered if I might like them. From the photo she sent, I thought they would be comfortable. My wife said they "looked like me". I sure hope that meant I was beginning to resemble an old shoe rather than a worn-out boot—not that I'm showing my age, mind you, other than my white hair.

I will also say that I'm perfectly fine with hand-me-downs. I wear them, drive in one, sleep under the roof of another, and I have always considered the earth the ultimate hand-me-down. I, too, am sort of a hand-me-down, sent out by my parents to be tried on and worn by the world. Some may keep me. Others may give me to Goodwill.

Ultimately, our text exchange didn't end up being about boots—I'm going to try them on and they'll probably end up in my closet. It was about the auto-correct function on my Google Pixel 2. The phone had belonged to my son, who announced a few months ago that he no longer wanted a smartphone. He said it was controlling too much of his life. He tossed it for a flip-phone, or old-school technology, as some would say. I caught it in mid-air. Why let such good technology go to waste? A hand-me-down from Google—ha! There's a first time for everything.

I remember back in the early eighties, with a good chuckle, how my mother announced she would never have an answering machine because she didn't want to be obligated to call anyone back. By then, she had grown weary of all the solicitation calls Dad was getting, asking for money. As much as I was moving into the future, she would simply have none of it. It took a hell of a lot of convincing to get her to even accept caller ID. The argument that persuaded her was that if she didn't recognize the number, she didn't have to answer the phone—and that included calls from her children. I think the latter might have convinced her. My God, when I consider the progress of technology since then, I think we are being consumed little by little by bits and bytes.

Okay, back to auto-correct and the attic. Alice started our text exchange and it went like this:

Alice: What size are your feet?

Me: Nine or nine and a half depending on the shoe.

Alice: Any interest in these shoes?

Me: Tracy says they look like me so I should at least try them on.

Alice: Sounds good. I am cleaning out some closets and donating some of our old stuff to the clothing bank.

> Me: Me too. I cleaned out my attitude.
> Some stuff has been in there for ten years
> untouched.

I intended to say "attic", but my Pixel 2 had different thoughts. But, simple auto-correct got me thinking: How many of my attitudes are old and worn out? Have I left them in the attic of my mind too long, only to gather dust? Are they hand-me-downs that need to be thrown out? Was it time to toss the bad and make space for the good? Could an attitude-cleaning help me be a better husband, father, friend, brother, son, neighbor, and citizen?

When I think of attics, I remember the one in my Dad's boyhood home in West Frankfort, Illinois. Accessible by a rickety stairway, it once held his old baseball cards, navy uniform, many memories of his early life, all packed away above that old house. Accessible by a rickety stairway, I vividly remember being in awe of all the stuff in that hide-away above the world. It held so many things, including those that once anchored Dad to his youth in the region of southern Illinois known as Little Egypt. In time he escaped his pharaoh—the baseball cards were tossed by his mom, the navy uniforms were eaten by moths, and the house on St. Louis Street was eventually demolished. There weren't seven plagues or the parting of the Red Sea: he drove his 1953 Ford convertible out of West Frankfort, left Little Egypt and headed east. His Promised Land, his land of milk and honey, lay across the Wabash River in Indiana. He drove his convertible over the Memorial Bridge that carried Highway 50 over the river, but unlike Moses, he reached his Promised Land.

Attics can be dusty places, full of stuff you don't know whether to keep or throw away. I think of attics as an earthly purgatory, where the material possessions and memories of one's life are stuck in limbo. Sometimes, I think it's a good thing to climb the stairs of my attic, push open the trap door, blow off the dust, and throw out the old attitudes.

Twelve Things That Made Me Happy This Week

For every minute you are angry you lose sixty seconds of happiness.

— Ralph Waldo Emerson

Recently, I was looking at my school picture from fourth grade and I wondered if I had lost *that* smile: the smile of pure joy that is childhood's gift—the same innocent and untainted beam I see on the face of my nine-year-old daughter, Sarah. I'd like to be mindful of moments in my adult life that should evoke such a smile.

These days, the happiness required for such an expression seems a bit harder to find. To use a well-worn simile, it's like trying to find a needle in a haystack. I'm not really an unhappy person, but I find that happiness is often easily overwhelmed by gloom.

To combat such disparity, I thought I would try a mental experiment that might help me better recognize those happy moments and resist the gloom and doom that may be lurking about. I chose to define my day by the number of things that made me smile, instead of the things that pissed me off.

I began by looking at my life like a chest of drawers: my favorite clothes are on top, and the stuff I don't wear or like so much lies at the bottom. This exercise required a serious mental rearrangement. I had to shove the things that really pissed me off into the bottom drawer, into the back of my mind, and place those things that made me happy at the forefront of my awareness. I could go cliché here and talk about wearing a smile instead of a frown, but I won't. I still frown, every day. By this experiment, I wanted to see if life's less comfortable garments could remain at the bottom of the drawer for a little while longer.

It was a real challenge, but it forced me to focus on the positive and not the negative. In the end, it was quite rewarding, and I am now making myself do it every day. I recognize those moments of happiness more frequently and am better at fighting off the gloom that tries to seep through. Whenever I reach down into the bottom of the drawer and don that black shirt of negativity, it doesn't stay on for long. It's not fitting well these days.

I started my first week with a rather modest approach. I decided that I would identify twelve things that made me smile over the course of seven days. Remember the "Twelve Days of Christmas"? I was intent on packing all those swimming swans, milking maids and leaping lords into a seven-day interval. I realized in the process that there were more than just twelve things that made me happy, but here are the first twelve:

1. My twenty-three-year-old son hugged me and told me he loved me.
2. My nine-year-old daughter told me that I was her favorite dad.

3. I heard cardinals singing every morning when I walked outside to collect the morning paper.
4. I went on a hike Sunday morning in Brown County State Park with my sons.
5. I looked at a picture of my late mother and father and realized how damn lucky I am to be their son.
6. I drove down the street where I lived as a child.
7. I heard sandhill cranes calling as they flew overhead towards their northern breeding grounds.
8. I rescued a bat that was trapped in my office building and released it outdoors.
9. I helped my son preserve a colony of honeybees in a tree that had been cut down on his mother's property.
10. My daffodils are ready to bloom.
11. I read Chinese poetry from the Tang Dynasty.
12. I talked to Mike, our mailman, just shooting the breeze.

...I am anxious for the next twelve.

By being mindful and seeking smiles during the past week, I did my damnedest to shrug my shoulders when the bad things happened. Bad people will always be around, hatred and racism will always exist, shit will always happen, mistakes will be made—and sometimes I'll still get pissed off.

Writing about the beauty in everyday life is cathartic. It won't silence the bad people or the demagogues, but perhaps my voice will be joined by others who seek love and beauty. It's a simple start to living a life that traffics less in gloom and more in joyful awareness.

Friday would have been my father's ninety-first

birthday. I lit candles in his honor and celebrated the man who lived his life in service to others. I gazed at pictures of my late parents in the candlelight. Rather than being sad at their passing, I thanked God for how lucky I was to have been born of these two wonderful people. I vowed to do my best to make my life reflect their lessons of selflessness and love. I will choose my daily raiment with care and make smiles the current fashion.

Clodhoppers

clod•hop•per (ˈklädˌhäpər) n.
1. a clumsy boor; rustic; bumpkin.
2. clodhoppers, strong, heavy shoes.
Source: Dictionary.com

L et me first dispel the notion that I'm a clumsy boor or a bumpkin, although I might appear a bit rustic to some. I find "down-to-earth" to be a more fitting descriptor. Too much society has never been my thing, and the older I get, the farther away from it I want to be. There are those who relish a crowd, but I head for the woods when I see one coming. I enjoy good company in measured doses, and without any pretense. But I digress: this is about clodhoppers, not society. Note that I use boots and clodhoppers interchangeably. A clodhopper has always been a boot to me, not a person.

My old boots had sat in the back corner of the closet, somewhat out of sight and a little out of mind, until the storm hit. Earlier this summer, we had a rather violent thunderstorm pass through with straight-line winds better than fifty miles an hour. I was in the backyard, tending my garden, when the storm arrived with a vengeance. "Vengeance is mine," saith the storm, and you'd better believe it. Discretion being the better part of valor, I beat a hasty retreat indoors.

At the peak of the storm, I heard the tell-tale *WHUMMPPP* of a large object hitting the ground. I "felt" the sound more than I heard it. When the storm subsided, I found our sugar maple down in the yard, its branches stretching across Royal Street. Being a somewhat anal person (just ask my wife), I wanted the tree removed as quickly as possible, and knowing that the city would already be overwhelmed with the storm's damage, I decided to tackle it on my own.

After putting on a pair of Levi's, I dug my clodhoppers out of the closet and put them on for the first time in over thirty-four years. With a pair of leather work gloves on my hands, I fired up my Stihl Farm Boss. Sawing into the wood reminded me of the days when I cut firewood for my dad's wood stove. I reveled in the feel of the boots on my feet, the chainsaw in my hands, the smell of the wood chips, and the sweat and satisfaction of hard work.

I think I got my first pair of clodhoppers when I was seven or eight: Redwings. The boots of my youth explored woods, farms, went on backpacking trips and Boy Scout campouts. They went with me on epic family camping trips to Maine, Wyoming, Virginia, and points beyond. As I grew older, they labored with me on land survey crews and at construction sites in places like East Chicago, New Washington, Pleasant Valley, and Whiting. These were the times that I learned about working hard and having fun at the same time. I got a hell of a lot of dirt on my clodhoppers through the years.

My boots became a part of my identity. I wore them five days a week, sunrise to sunset. I religiously rubbed beeswax into the leather to keep it soft, waterproof, and comfortable on my feet. Then as now, they fit me like a glove. Eventually, I moved on to a new chapter in my life and traded them for dress shoes. But I couldn't bring myself to let them go, so they followed me through the years to my closet here on Roselawn Avenue. Looking back, I enjoyed wearing my clodhoppers a lot more—my dress shoes always felt a bit stiff and unforgiving.

When I look at my old clodhoppers, I see the young man who wore them so many years ago, and I realize that I am not much changed: a few more aches and pains for sure, but flesh, bone, and spirit all remain. The weathered leather of my boots mirrors the lines on my face. Together, they tell my story.

Lost in Time

Sometimes I get lost in the woods. Not lost in a physical sense, for I have always found my way home. My "lost" is more of a state of mind in which I become so absorbed in my environment and the moment that I lose track of time. The natural world is a way to escape what Nessmuk called the "debts, duns, and deviltries" of life.

There are certain prerequisites that must exist, I think, if one is to get "lost". First, you must be in the right frame of mind. You must be willing to walk away from those things in your life that are weighing heavy on your mind. Work, money, personal relationships, the past and the future must be left behind. Next, you must find the right place. It could be your backyard, but more likely it will be that special place in the state park, a canoe trip down the river, or the woods of a friend—a place you can go and enjoy some moments undisturbed in nature. It might happen while you are leaning against a tree, listening to the wind blowing through the branches. It might happen when you are stalking a deer or watching a squirrel darting about. Maybe it happens while you are observing the vibrant colors of fall or celebrating the new growth of spring. There are many such places and opportunities.

The next thing you needed is the right companion. Perhaps the best companion at the time is yourself.

Thoreau once said, "I have not yet met the companion as companionable as solitude." If someone joins you, they should be of like mind and temperament.

I think of it in the same way I would choose a canoe partner. Their paddle stroke must be compatible with my own and our conversation must flow easily and without effort. When we observe something, more often than not we need say nothing, for we both have the same feelings. We understand each other's likes and dislikes and our discourse reflects our similarities. At night, around the campfire, our conversation tends to be philosophical.

These are a few of the ingredients that I need in order to get "lost". I am sure each person has their own recipe. I urge you to take a walk in the woods. To paraphrase Thoreau, you might find a thousand regions of your mind yet unexplored.

The Art of Walking

Some take a stroll while others go for a hike. In Australia, they have the 'walkabout'. Woody Guthrie sang about roaming in his song, "Ramblin' Man":

> "My mother prayed that I would be
> A man of some renown
> But I'm just a railroad bum
> As I go ramblin' 'round boys
> As I go ramblin' 'round"

Henry David Thoreau wrote about sauntering in his essay, "Walking":

> "I have met with but one or two persons in the course of my life who understood the art of Walking, that is, of taking walks — who had a genius, so to speak, for sauntering, which word is beautifully derived "from idle people who roved about the country, in the Middle Ages, and asked charity, under pretense of going a la Sainte Terre, to the Holy Land, till the children exclaimed, "There goes a Sainte-Terrer," a Saunterer, a Holy-Lander. They who never go to the Holy

Land in their walks, as they pretend, are indeed mere idlers and vagabonds; but they who do go there are saunterers in the good sense, such as I mean. Some, however, would derive the word from sans terre, without land or a home, which, therefore, in the good sense, will mean, having no particular home, but equally at home everywhere. For this is the secret of successful sauntering. He who sits still in a house all the time may be the greatest vagrant of all; but the saunterer, in the good sense, is no more vagrant than the meandering river, which is all the while sedulously seeking the shortest course to the sea."

Walt Whitman wrote about perambulation:

"In our sun-down perambulations, of late, through the outer parts of Brooklyn, we have observed several parties of youngsters playing base, a certain game of ball...Let us go forth awhile, and get better air in our lungs. Let us leave our close rooms..."

Like Thoreau, I like to saunter, seek out my Holy Land, but I am equally at home with a good perambulation. The Oxford Dictionary says that to "perambulate" means "to walk or travel through or around a place or area, especially for pleasure and in a leisurely way." Merriam-Webster adds that it involves "making an official inspection on foot".

In *Walden*, Thoreau writes,

> "For many years I was self-appointed inspector of snow-storms and rain-storms, and did my duty faithfully; surveyor, if not of highways, then of forest paths and all across-lot routes, keeping them open, and ravines bridged and passable at all seasons, where the public heel had testified to their utility."

When I am out in the woods, I prefer a leisurely stroll that allows me to make a close inspection of those things around me. I often go perambulating or sauntering in Brown County State Park. In any moment, I am the self-appointed inspector of woodland ponds, wildflowers, budding trees, rippling streams, birds, box turtles, gray squirrels, chipmunks, and insects. I do not merely walk through the woods; rather, I walk in them. They become a part of me and each step is a new discovery. I never feel more alive than I do in these moments. I am in my Holy Land, among the sacred, and in the presence of God. To saunter or perambulate means to walk with a spirit-sense, where each step has meaning and results in continuing revelations of nature's divine beauty. The greatest adventure of my life has been my voyage of self-discovery in the natural world. I will continue to go to the woods with no destination in mind, no race to run, but merely to learn what nature has to teach.

A Winter Walk

I am sitting here at my desk listening to the wind howling outside my window: I love that sound. It evokes the deepest thoughts from my soul. Earlier this evening, I took a walk through the empty, snow-covered streets, staring at the evening lights shining from the houses, but not a person stirring. I felt as an interloper—or perhaps more like an adventurer—braving the snow and cold to soak in the loneliness of a winter storm. The wind and snow made me hunker down as I made my way through the silent streets, glad I had dressed for the occasion. My footprints will be gone tomorrow, blown away by the wind, but each step will be with me as a memory, carrying me back to my solitary adventure in winter's domain.

The Road Taken

But great grand schemes will give you grief.
Take what you need, that's all. A light craft
takes the wind and skims the water lightly.

Last verse from "Writing What I've Seen"
by Yuan Mei (1716-1798)

Many of you have known me for years, and some of you are more recent acquaintances. Let me say that I appreciate and love you all, for as much as I like being alone, I also love the company of friends and family. This is a wonderful mix of social skills given to me by my father and late mother. Dad loves to be around people and knows no stranger, while my mother could be in a crowd but much preferred an intimate gathering with close friends and family, or simply being alone. I am a mix of both, but in the end, aren't we really a product of both our parents, like it or not?

As I have said, I gained a love of nature early in life. Whether barefoot on a summer day, going into the country with my grandfather and catching frogs or fishing, on Boy Scout campouts or on summer road trips with my family, backpacking into the wilderness with Dad—through it all

I gained a love of nature and embraced all its facets. That love remains as much a part of my soul as my dearest friends.

Too soon, the carefree days of my boyhood ended and with adulthood came the expectations of building a career and starting a family. As I look back on this transition, I sometimes regret that I didn't follow my passion for nature and pursue a career in natural resources. Instead, I allowed myself to be sucked into the American expectation of success and money. I have many things for which I am thankful: four children and a WONDERFUL wife. The things that eluded me were more intellectual or spiritual. I had the material necessities: a good home, a six-figure salary. I bought shit when I needed it, albeit not a larger home or a second home, a fancy car or a Gucci wallet. I plowed my way up the food chain while I watched others around me struggle to meet the ever-demanding expectations of corporate life. Some fell away like chaff. I began to see the hypocrisy of that existence and asked myself if there wasn't something better. It all came crashing down not yet a year ago, but I crawled out from the destruction and I have never been happier.

Here I am now, writing my heart out about nature, spending some fantastic time with my girls, Katie and Sarah, taking them to school and being with them at the end of the day. I do the cooking, cleaning, and grocery shopping (I love you Mom—you set the example). My adult sons have a new level of respect as I have eschewed the mindless pursuit of money and status. A year ago, I never imagined I would be in this place, but I know this: I will never go back. This Old Boy is happy where he is.

While "The Man" demands more from those around me, I may be taking a weekday hike in the woods. While others fight crowded airports to travel to their next rendezvous or drink in some lonely airport bar, I may be cracking open a beer and sitting in my Adirondack chair in my backyard, staring up at the blue sky, listening to Dylan or the Doors. I am not envious of those hungry for the next dollar. I can only imagine what their lives would be like if they took a step back and asked the question, "Am I happy where I am? Has it all been worth the getting?" It's a question we all will answer, sooner or later.

There Was No Gate

"The Great Way has no gate, A thousand roads enter it. When one passes through this gateless gate, He freely walks between heaven and earth."

From "The Gateless Gate" by Mumon (1228 AD)

In Brown County State Park, about a quarter mile past Weed Patch Hill, there is a simple wooden gate along the road that marks the start of a path heading south into the woods. I have passed it many times, never stopping, somehow feeling the gate was there to prevent my entry. As the path beyond it disappeared into the woods, I would often wonder where it led and what natural or spiritual revelations there might be along the way. Just a few days ago, I finally overcame my misguided apprehension, swung open the gate and walked through.

As I walked into the woods, a hazy fog lay close to the ground, obscuring more distant views. A light mist wet my hair and jacket. Small droplets of water, heaven's dew, clung to the trees and I tasted a few drops rolling down the branch of a beech tree. I became oblivious to how wet I was and instead watched intently as each of my footsteps sank into the wet leaves that carpeted the ground. I soon became lost in time, no longer thinking about my watch, where I came from, or where I had to be. As I became totally absorbed in the moment, life's challenges suddenly seemed inconsequential; nature enfolded me in her arms and my spirit soared through the woodlands.

Soon, it felt like I was in a rainforest rather than the temperate climate of Indiana. The moisture hung heavy in the air, the brown bark of the trees was painted green, brown, and white by lichens. Rotting logs lay on the woodland floor, returning to the soil from where they came. A variety of mosses dotted the woods, each with its own color and texture. The smell of decaying leaves rose from the ground.

Continuing along a ridgeline, I heard the sound of flowing water as two streams began their journey to the valley floor. The water, flowing over the exposed sandstone bedrock, created small waterfalls that added to nature's melody, a beautiful sound that never failed to enchant me. As I reached the valley floor, I was so enthralled by the moment that I walked back up each stream a ways to explore their finer details.

Then, following the main stream, I soon realized I was in familiar territory, having walked it many times and in all seasons. It is in spring, though, that I find it most enjoyable as the flowing water brings the woods to life. Finally, catching a glimpse of the back side of Strahl Lake, I was soon walking the familiar path around its shoreline. The unknown had become the known.

Ending my descent into the valley at the abandoned shelter house at the lake, I broke bread: a brunch of cheese, bread, and salami. Topping it off with a nice crisp apple, I settled back for a moment and reflected on my morning.

I thought of how blessed I have been in my life to have nature as a source of renewal, of rebirth, a guide when I needed new focus. My descent through these wooded hills and into the valley required me to swing open a gate and enter a place I had never explored. I experienced that magical moment when my body, mind, and soul were bound together by nature's golden thread. In the end, I really didn't need to physically push open the gate at the top of the hill—I simply walked around it. I need to free myself from building gates and let life take me where it wants.

Source:
Yamada, Kōun. *The Gateless Gate*, The Classic Book of Zen Koans, Wisdom Publications, 2015.

When I Hike Alone, I Prefer to be By Myself (with apologies to George Thorogood)

I had three chairs in my house; one for solitude, two for friendship, three for society.

– Henry David Thoreau, *Walden*

I have always been an introvert and have cultivated this quality carefully throughout my life, lest I appear too anti-social. It's a delicate dance. Don't get me wrong, I will always enjoy the company of family and friends, but there are times when I prefer to be alone. I often prefer my only company to be the trees, birds, and squirrels. When I am alone in the woods, I am much more introspective because I slow down and immerse myself in my surroundings. There is no idle chat, no material distractions; my focus is in the moment. I am in my mind. Being alone is also a gut-check on whether I like my own company. If I can't get along with me, whom else can I get along with?

I have some wonderful hiking partners and enjoy excursions with each of them, but I have always lived by the creed that a hiking partner must be chosen with the same criteria as a canoe mate. Being in a canoe once with someone whose paddle strokes were incompatible with my own totally wore me out. I tried to compensate and keep the canoe going straight, but instead it became less like a boat and more like a bee, zig-zagging from flower to flower. Coupling that with a personality that didn't much mesh with my own, I just wanted to jump out and swim for shore. There have been times when I have passed people in the woods and thought, if I were with them, I would run away screaming for my life. I have had similar experiences at cocktail parties and other social gatherings.

This past Wednesday morning, I had the opportunity to escape society for a bit and take a walk in the woods. It was an exceptionally beautiful day as the spring wildflowers were beginning to bloom: bloodroot, spring beauties, cut-leaf toothwort, Dutchman's breeches and violets dotted the forest floor. The sun gave me that sense of well-being it provides on a warm day after a period of cold and wet weather. A strong wind stirred the treetops and its low roar serenaded me as I wandered among the trees. The streams flowed and the chickadees, titmice, and other woodland birds flitted through the understory. I sat down on an old log at the edge of a ravine and enjoyed a mid-morning coffee and snack. A cup of coffee with oneself, while savoring the beauty of the woods, is singularly fulfilling. No Starbucks drive-through can create such nectar. My mind soared as free and clear as the wind and the sky.

Much too soon I had to tear myself away from solitude and head down the trail, back to society. I had just spent three hours alone in the woods and was at peace with the world. As I drove home, I began plotting my next excursion; these solitary escapes will always remain a part of my earthly life. In solitude, I can explore the deepest reaches of my being, blow away the dust of the world, and discover something new and exciting about myself. It is also an opportunity to nurture my introvert, who is as much a part of me as my blue eyes and gray hair. Meaningful solitude for me is a constant: it dares me to be alone, to throw off the yoke of expectations, and explore myself at depths unattainable in a crowd.

Solitude is not something you must hope for in the future. Rather, it is a deepening of the present, and unless you look for it in the present you will never find it.

- Thomas Merton

A Story of Perseverance

"Endeavor to persevere." These words have stuck with me since I first heard them in the 1976 movie *The Outlaw Josey Wales*, starring Clint Eastwood. They are spoken by the character Lone Watie, played by Chief Dan George. Endeavor to persevere, try hard to overcome a seemingly insurmountable obstacle in the face of extreme difficulty. Stay the course, press on, and do one's damnedest when the odds are long.

It's hard for me to believe that it's been a little over ten years since my wife and I lost our home to the catastrophic flood that inundated Columbus, Indiana on June 7, 2008. I have been reticent about putting the events of that summer into words, feeling my emotions were still too raw and, quite frankly, wanting to forget that it ever happened. However, the passing of time has assuaged the anguish of that experience and I can now view it with a bit more ease.

The day of the flood dawned rainy and, as we stirred, my wife and I had no idea of the physical and mental challenges that would face us in a few short hours. It continued raining into the afternoon, but by late in the day the clouds had cleared and the sun finally peeked through. We had eaten dinner out and returned home to a lot of commotion in our neighborhood, known as The Lagoons. Neighbors were out in their yards, walking up and down the street, eyes wide with panic as the Flatrock River, a few hundred yards away, was overflowing its banks. My wife and I walked to nearby Noblitt Park to view the river: we watched as the waters headed right for us. When I returned to my house, I walked to the end of the street where the river was less than a block from our door. When I turned to look north, up Flatrock Drive, I did a double-take: a foot-high wall of water was rolling towards me. Soon, the muddy waters passed me up as I ran for my house. We were about to experience what they called a "Hundred-Year-Flood".

I burst through the front door and shouted for Tracy to carry what we could out of the basement. I remember seeing the window well filling up with water and thinking, *Damn, this isn't going to be good.* Fortunately, our home was a tri-level, so we used the upper part as a repository for many of our belongings. We also had a walkout basement for easy access to the lagoon, which came into play later on. We carried as much as we could while caring for our two-year old daughter, Katie. As water cascaded down the basement steps from the main level, I felt it prudent to send my wife and daughter to higher ground. My ex-wife, Jeannie, graciously welcomed them into her home.

After seeing them safely off, I continued to work feverishly into the evening, with water beginning to rise against the basement door. Sweat and floodwater joined together. I continued working as the sun faded away, wading through thigh-deep water, bent on a mission of preservation. Almost in a trance, I carried books, baseball cards, record albums, tools, family pictures, and childhood memories up the steps. It felt like something out of an old submarine movie, with jets of water spraying through the basement door as the water rose outside. With the water now waist deep, the door could no longer hold. The jam splintered, the door blew open and with it came a wall of water. I didn't realize I could move so fast, but I flew up the steps to the main level. With darkness and a feeling of dread overwhelming me, I put a leash on our golden retriever, Lizzy, and waded out into the flooded streets. Catching a ride in a friend's truck, Lizzy and I left a surreal scene and went to join my wife and child, wondering what the morning would bring.

I vividly remember waking up the next day, a bright and sunny Sunday, looking out my ex's window and seeing a woman walking her dog. It struck me that she was probably oblivious to the events of the previous night: her life was unchanged. I knew instinctively that my life was already changed—just how much, I couldn't yet imagine.

When I returned to my house that Sunday, I was overwhelmed: the mud, the ruined furniture, the deck wrenched from its posts, dead fish in the front yard, a water snake in my terrace garden, and water lapping at the top of the steps leading into the basement. So much more lay hidden, to be revealed once the floodwaters had receded.

It wasn't the way I had planned to do late-spring cleaning, but I had no choice. As the pile of ruined household items grew, so did the sense of loss. Mind you, I use the term "ruined" and not "destroyed". Fire destroys, water ruins. I knew intimately every item I threw on the pile in the driveway. But it was the mud that drove me crazy: it found its way into every nook and cranny, every square inch of what we had left—driven deep into the crevices of our souls. Years later, we would still find a spot of mud on something we had salvaged, a reminder of those agonizing days.

Eventually, the water was pumped out of The Lagoons and, after an emotional and draining clean-up, we faced the myriad regulatory and insurance issues of owning a home on the floodplain. Fortunately, we had mandatory flood insurance, so all would not be a total loss. But the state said, for us to occupy the house, the main floor would have to be raised three feet above the 100-year flood level—at an unimaginable cost. After several trips to the city planning department, I felt like I had been backed into a corner.

Tracy and I were faced with the question: should we stay or should we go? After huddling together, we felt that we could no longer live with the possibility of another flood. We had to chart a future away from this place, even though it was our first home together. After some back-and-forth with the insurance company, we were able to have the property declared a total loss and received the full amount available under our flood insurance. We put the house on the market and found a cash buyer. With these proceeds, we were able to pay off our existing mortgage and have a cash balance: a victory after so much loss.

We eventually moved into temporary housing and, while there, befriended the couple across the hall. Rajesh and Geetha were from India and living in Columbus while he worked on a project at Cummins Engine Company. We ate Indian food many evenings and Rajesh and I shared more than a little Kentucky bourbon on those summer nights. Through the simple acts of breaking bread and sipping a little bourbon, we learned a hell of a lot about the common bonds that bring humankind together.

Whether it was the support of our parents and siblings, friends lending a hand, temporary lodging provided by my ex-wife, co-workers helping pack up our remaining belongings, our pastor supplying some cold beer when I needed it most, my sons standing beside their dad, or the total strangers who lent a hand, we reaffirmed the importance of all of the people in our lives. We were touched by many people that summer, both seen and unseen, each one a reminder of the complex weave of human relationships. To separate ourselves from it would have been folly.

We now live in a new home a couple of miles north of The Lagoons. I ride my bike to Parkside Elementary School in the morning with my daughter, Sarah, and I'm home in the afternoon when the bus drops off Katie from another day in seventh grade. I have a wonderful garden where I grow tomatoes, herbs, and peppers. I have wildflowers that attract beautiful butterflies and I feed the birds—and consequently a lot of squirrels. I say hello to my neighbors and know them by name. My sons often play pitch and catch in the yard and our daughters swing under the sycamore tree. I chat with our mailman and always greet our UPS guy. Living here now feels like a natural progression, no longer like a forced march: it is like there was no place else we were meant to be.

Watching an ant colony going about its business has always fascinated me. What might first appear as chaos is in truth very orderly and well-defined. I had an old bird box in the backyard that fell from the cherry tree a few weeks ago. When I knocked out the old nest material, a colony of small black ants emerged, along with hundreds of their tiny eggs. When I came back a while later, the ants and their eggs had completely disappeared. They had survived the destruction of their home and moved on to reestablish it someplace else.

Ten summers ago, we also faced the destruction of our home. We lived through it all, we lost, and we gained. We are survivors. We love life, with all its twists and turns, and will always remember that we did our damnedest and endeavored to persevere when the odds were against us.

Twists and Turns

What lies behind us and what lies ahead of us are tiny matters compared to what lives within us.

- Variously Attributed

Life has never really turned out quite like I planned, and most days I can't even remember whether I had a plan. I'm not complaining, since things have turned out pretty well in spite of my best efforts to the contrary. I quit listening to the cacophony of advice some time ago, the "you need to do this" or "you need to do that"—and there never has been a shortage of "this" and "that". I don't need motivational speakers, podcasts, or self-help books to guide me. I don't need to know the five easy ways to guaranteed success, how to get rich quick without even trying, or the "art of the deal". Hell, if I read or listened to all the prophets who are sure they know the secret to my success, I would be so confused that I'd never get out of bed in the morning. Often, my life feels more like I scattered a handful of seeds in a garden, not knowing what would emerge—but that has been the beauty of my adventure.

A little over fifty-five years ago, my mother walked me a few blocks from home to Schmitt Elementary for my first day of kindergarten. I am sure we held hands and she gave me a kiss and a hug as Mrs. Moore welcomed me to her classroom. I'm also sure I was excited about what lay ahead, but also scared of the unknown—and, I do know I missed my mom. I still do. At some point, the innocence of childhood gave way to the responsibilities of being a grown-up. With it came the ups and downs of living, some of which have gone the way I planned, and some not so much. But through it all, I have held close the child in me, and he serves as a constant reminder not to take life too seriously and to never lose that sense of wonder.

I never ask for do-overs. Every decision, every choice I have made has had a ripple effect in my life. To go back in time and change things would be to disrupt the flow of events that have brought me to this moment. Through jobs changed and lost, divorce, marriage, flood, children, easy decisions or tough decisions, every move I made resulted in different outcomes that led me to this moment. Sometimes I ponder, "what if?": What if I had taken that job? What if I had not gone to college? What if I'd married that other girl? What if I had no children? This is a mere academic exercise rather than a wish, for what's done is done. As I sit here on the backside of life, I don't pine for "what if"; I look forward to what is yet to come.

The adventure of life is seeing what grows from a single seed. What random collection of events strung together will cause a paradigm shift, a radical altering of life's trajectory? What will come from that experience, the decision made or not made? Or, will things just continue as before? Just as the plant grows and spreads out its roots, my roots also have spread out into the new soil of my life's experiences. As I grow older and my flower begins to fade a bit, my roots are a tangle of memories: paths taken, decisions made, and ultimately the consequences of life. I look back with no regrets, no wishes for things to be different. Life is what it is and the only thing I can change, perhaps, is tomorrow. But tomorrow will come in a few short hours; a few more seeds will be scattered in my garden and I will wonder what will sprout. Without question, my younger self will be with me when I awaken, to remind me that life is fun and there is a world out there yet to be explored.

Dreams

I learned this, at least, by my experiment: that if one advances confidently in the direction of his dreams, and endeavors to live the life which he has imagined he will meet with a success unexpected in common hours...If you have built castles in the air, your work need not be lost; that is where they should be. Now put the foundations under them."

- Henry David Thoreau, *Walden*

When first asked as a boy what I wanted to be when I grew up, I am sure I said a fireman. That was what a boy my age was expected to say, even though I wasn't really serious. The first occupation I recall having serious thoughts about was being a Major League baseball player. The seeds of that dream were sown when I first started watching ball games on black and white TV with my grandfather. I couldn't imagine a better job: the glory of victory, a ninth inning home run to win the game, striking out the side to win the World Series. I would be idolized, the Hall of Fame sure to follow.

I also remember the exact moment when my hopes and dreams of glory on the baseball diamond were dashed to bits on the rocks of reality.

I had been playing Little League baseball for a few years and imagined myself much better than I actually was. I was maybe ten or eleven at the time, sitting in the back seat of my parents' car with my older sister, when my dad asked me what I wanted to be when I grew up. We were heading south on Washington Street in Columbus, between ninth and eighth streets, when I confidently stated that I would be pitching for the St. Louis Cardinals—to which my sister then replied, with just as much confidence, that I would never play professional baseball because I was no good. At least she had the decency not to say that I sucked. I was devastated, but realized she was right: when you pray for rain on game day and have only collected three hits in your "professional" career, you had better come up with an alternative life plan.

This began the period of my life that I call the "desert" of my dreams. I wandered into high school with some vague idea of what I liked and didn't, but I was really more interested in screwing off and avoiding getting caught for various shenanigans. It wasn't until my senior year that I decided I wanted to be a forest ranger, the batteries of career tests I went through suggesting that I might be on to something. When I told my parents of this great revelation, my dad's immediate response was, "Why would you do that? You'll never make any money." Being the acquiescent son, I immediately abandoned that dream and reentered the desert. I have to admit, though, that my grades and overall motivation at the time probably wouldn't have carried me too far. Reality can douse a lot of fires.

So, I wandered, mostly looking for fun rather than a

future. I eventually completed college, graduating with a degree in political science from Indiana University in 1986. I then worked for the Governor of Indiana, was Director of Marketing for an insurance company, worked for my father's engineering firm, and spent over twelve years as Director of Human Resources for a local company. Through all those years, the dream of being a forest ranger hovered in the back of my mind. I have found that dreams don't die; they sometimes just have different endings.

As I was preparing to start a new role in human resources in 2005, I sought the advice of a career counselor. The results were eye-opening: they suggested that I had nothing in common with people who were in human resources. I had more in common, they told me, with people who wrote about natural history. I wasn't surprised by the results, as HR didn't get me overly excited; it just seemed to be the best way to leverage my talents in order to make decent money. I had no real passion for it. I did it for other reasons and probably for all the wrong ones. Sometimes, I think I sold my soul to the devil that is money. But, the Fates shined on me a little over a year ago and I escaped the devil's clutches.

About nine years ago, I was staring at my bookshelves and all the natural history guides I had collected over the years. I recall thinking, *Why don't you do something with these? They're just gathering dust.* At that moment the idea of "Upon Common Ground" was born, and I published my first newsletter that fall. There have been more than a few fits and starts along the way, and I continue to grow and mature as a writer. I am often my own worst critic, never really feeling a piece is the best it can be. But

I keep on doing it because of the deep satisfaction that I get from painting pictures with words.bucket list

I'll soon be sixty—it's too late to don that St. Louis Cardinals uniform and play in the Major Leagues. I'm not a forest ranger, either, but I found my way back to that dream—the ending is just a little different. It's not my day job, but I walk in the woods as often as I can and never miss a chance to observe nature, even if it's just outside my door. I would have never dreamed, sitting in the back seat of that car on Washington Street all those years ago, that I would be sitting here typing these words. What I have learned from my own experience is to advance confidently in the direction of my dream and welcome each success, big or small, whatever the hour. I still have a lot of words to share and pictures to paint.

My Bucket List

I don't have a "bucket list". I've grown a bit weary of the phrase, "One hundred things to do or places to go before you die". I think we often just *do* places, we don't really *experience* them. Take a selfie, then on to the next stop—another item checked off the list. Did this, did that, done. By treating life as a checklist, we lose its sanctity. Places and things are meant to be experienced, embraced, and not just passed through. In our effort to pack in as much as possible, we become disconnected from the world and those around us. We don't stop and smell the roses anymore.

I Googled "Bucket List" and found hundreds of links, twenty-six pages to be exact. I quit looking after ten, but here are just a few of the sites:

- Bucket List Ideas: 101 Things To Do Before You Die
- Unique Bucket List: 1000+ Ideas — Live the Dream - Bucket List Journey
- Bucket List: The Ultimate Guide to Creating Your Bucket List Right Now
- Bucketlist – 10,000 things to do before you die
- Bucket List: 100+ Incredible Things to Do Before You Die
- The Bucket List – Wikipedia

- 43 Places to add To Your 2019 Bucket List
- 12 Things That Aren't on Your Bucket List (But Should Be) | MyDomaine
- 329 Bucket List Ideas To Try and Thing [sic] To Do Before You Die

"Google" them and enjoy, or be overwhelmed.

Ten thousand things, let alone even a thousand! If I tried to do a thousand things, I'd either be in debtor's prison or die trying, succumbing to hypothermia on the slopes of Mt. Everest or dysentery in some tropical locale. They even made a movie, *The Bucket List*, starring Jack Nicholson and Morgan Freeman; and no, I haven't seen it.

The only thing on my bucket list is kicking the bucket—that's one thing I'm sure to accomplish. But I'm not quite ready yet. I've got plans between now and then, such as spending some quality time with my family and going for quite a few walks in the woods. But my list isn't in or written on some bucket. Who invented the bucket list anyway? Perhaps it was someone with either a lot of time on their hands, a pile of money, or something to sell. I find lists to be self-defeating and often downright depressing. Why would I put down "walk on the moon" or "summit Mt. Everest", if I knew it would never happen? Some would say, "Dreams, you have to have dreams". If I had a thousand things on a list, nine hundred I knew I could never accomplish, I would end up cowering in a corner, suffering from a nervous breakdown.

I do have places I want to go and things I want to do. But I also know there will be things that are out of reach, dreams that will fade with the morning light, and mountains that will remain unclimbed. When I think of a bucket, I think of mopping the floor or cleaning up a mess. Sometimes the mess is of my own making, and a little Mr. Clean sure comes in handy.

The things I want to accomplish have always been a little closer to home, not in some faraway province or ethereal realm. If I make the effort to explore my world, go for a walk in the woods, dig deep in my home ground, hug my wife and children, then perhaps my dreams will become celestial and last beyond the morning. I'm just lucky—lucky my life keeps my bucket full right where my butt's been planted. Unless I wake up sitting on the First National Bank, I'll just clean up around the house and go for a walk in the woods. When I walk out the door, my bucket will remain under the wash sink in the basement, where it belongs. My life is damn good.

II. FELLOW TRAVELERS

The Beauty of Words

Language is wine upon the lips.

-Virginia Woolf

Dad was a civil engineer (Missouri School of Mines and Metallurgy—Rolla, Class of '52). His engineering firm designed sewage treatment plants and he used to say, "It may be crap to you, but it's money to me." Within his lexicon were two words I remember well, *"sigogglin"* and *"cattywampus"*. For sure, they didn't come out of his structural engineering textbook; rather, I suspect he learned them from his father, who made his living as a carpenter. I imagine those words rolling easily off Grandpa's tongue, a Chesterfield cigarette dangling from his lips: *"You better measure that board twice and cut once, Kenneth, lest that wall turn out all sigogglin."*

Before I was old enough to know better, I thought *"sigogglin"* was a person named Cy Gogglin and *"cattywampus"* had something to do with herding cats. I eventually learned that Cy wasn't a person and that "cattywampus" had nothing to do with the feline persuasion. "Sigogglin", Appalachian in origin, means that something is built crooked, skewed, or out of balance, and

59

"cattywampus" most likely derived from the Scottish word *wampus*, means something is not lined up or arranged correctly. Whatever the disorder in my young life, I was on my way to discovering the richness of my family's lexicon.

My maternal grandfather and uncle grew up in the southern part of the county in what was then a German enclave in Waymansville. Their native tongue was German, and they learned English only when necessity forced them to assimilate into the Anglo-centric world. Attending school through the eighth grade, they lived close to the land. I always think of their language as being born of the soil. You could almost hold their words in your hands and feel the richness of their meaning.

You went down to the "crik" and "around the bend", and the cows were pastured down in the "holler." You "put up hay", and the air was "close" on a hot and humid August day. Plenty of something was a "right smart amount" and you could get "too much speed up" on the tractor. Things that were out of sight were, "down yonder". To "tax" something was to put too much stress on it, and being "work brittle" meant you were lazy. A board might be "purt near, but not plumb." That could go for you, too. Hogs were "slopped" and being "taken to the woodshed" wasn't where a wayward boy wanted to go. The Ohio River was "Big Waters" and hominy and grits were "good eats". There were city-folk and farmers. There were barn-raisings, community butcherings, and Sunday worship at St. Peter Lutheran Church. It was a community tied together by faith, language, and vocation.

Although well-educated, Dad's vocabulary had any number of idiosyncrasies, in large part influenced by his home ground. He grew up in southern Illinois, in the region they call "Little Egypt". This is where the city of Cairo isn't in Egypt and it's pronounced K-Ro. Eldorado doesn't lie "over the mountains of the moon" or "down in the valley of the shadow"; it's on Illinois 142. Equality is just down the road a way, Metropolis isn't the home of Superman, and Halfway is in the middle of nowhere. A doctor once tried to tell Dad it was "saline" solution and not "suh-lean" solution. He promptly replied, with emphasis, that he must not be from southern Illinois because it was called "Suh-lean", as in Saline County.

He was also a master at making up words, "ginkfod" being one of my favorites. "Straighten up and stop acting like a ginkfod," he would tell me. A "gink" is an odd boy, but I was never sure what a "fod" was. And as often as I told him it was regardless or irrespective, not irregardless, it made no difference. He would always say, with a wry smile, that the longest word in the English language was "supercalifragilisticexpialidocious".

I grew up around a richness of words, born of local influences, the sweat of hard work, and the unique characters of the people who spoke them. They weren't big, fancy words. They didn't have to be. They made their point. Their words were their histories, the places they came from and how they made a living. A simple conversation could be so rich in meaning, begging to be held onto, to be savored, sifted through your fingers like a handful of fine soil. I can still hear their words, floating through the air and into my eager ears.

The difference between the almost right word and the right word is really a large matter -- 'tis the difference between the lightning bug and the lightning.

—Mark Twain

My Muse

THERE is no architect
Can build as the Muse can;
She is skillful to select
Materials for her plan;

From *The House* by Ralph Waldo Emerson

D o you have a muse—someone or something that inspires you artistically? Maybe your muse compels you to write poetry, play a musical instrument, dance, or paint. When I first thought of myself as a writer, I hadn't really given much thought about a muse. Early on, there was a creative disconnect that existed between me and my subject. It felt as if I were only dipping my toe into the deep well of my being. Somehow, my thoughts became words, but there wasn't a feeling of giving myself up to my subject. I knew I needed to find my muse and fully embrace its influence on my mind and spirit.

For certain, my muse was never going to reveal itself between the hours of 8 and 5, Monday through Friday, unless I had the day off. Work, for the most part, has been a means to an end for me. There have been moments of satisfaction, but they came and went quickly. Throughout my life, "the grind" did more to separate me from my muse than to bring us together. I turned my back on my creativity and stumbled blindly into the relentless pursuit of money and status. The words of Henry David Thoreau served as my wake-up call:

> "The mass of men lead lives of quiet desperation. What is called resignation is confirmed desperation. From the desperate city you go into the desperate country, and have to console yourself with the bravery of minks and muskrats. A stereotyped but unconscious despair is concealed even under what are called the games and amusements of mankind. There is no play in them, for this comes after work. But it is the characteristic of wisdom not to do desperate things."

Often, these words scared me out of my wits when I pondered whether resignation and desperation would overwhelm me. They compelled me to search for a way by which I could be delivered from blind toil in pursuit of material gain. By grace and luck, I have chosen not to do desperate things and have taken a different path. The road has not been easy, but I am determined to stay the course and not allow resignation, desperation, and the relentless pursuit of money and status to be my epitaph.

My muse was never far. I found a spiritual haven in my garden: tilling the soil in spring, smelling the fresh earth, letting it run through my fingers, carefully placing seeds and plants in the earth to nurture them to maturity. Later, I enjoyed the fruits of my honest labors while watching butterflies and bumblebees visit the flowers. A variety of birds visited my feeders. My garden was a sanctuary, a place where I could escape the "deviltries", as Nessmuk wrote, of the day.

Just a few days ago, I hiked the Fire Tower Trail in Brown County State Park, a short but rugged 2.2-mile loop that meanders through a beautiful, hardwood landscape. It had rained during the night, so the trail was a bit sloppy and crossing a swollen creek required careful passage to avoid a soaking. These were but minor obstacles in the way of enjoying the peace of being in the woods. I stopped often to listen to the wind and watch the treetops sway back and forth in their ancient rhythms. I heard the soothing sound of the stream running full and watched its swirling currents rush by. The pale leaves of the beech trees rattled in the winter wind. Each pause filled my senses with joy, a pleasant reminder of why I had always sought out such places.

These moments—past, present and yet to come—allow me to turn inward and immerse myself in the deep well of my being. The common bond that ties them all together is nature, my muse, a fundamental part of my life since childhood. It is a mind-clearing experience to be with her. The dust of the world disappears, and she is at once nurturing, sensual, and beguiling. She invites me to explore her many moods and to embrace each as a friend and guide. When I am with her, I am like a child again, gazing in wonder at the natural world around me, giddy at the chance of discovering something that touches my very being. I am that boy who bounded out the door of his house, barefoot on a summer morning, in awe of the world around him, and who has yet to come back inside.

When I am in a creative lull and can't find the right words to express myself, I am always confident that a trip to the woods or garden to walk with my muse will provide what I seek. I am liberated by nature: she helps me remove the shackles of my daily life; she unfetters me from time and the myopic perspective that I too often force upon myself. With her, I dare to dream what I can be, rather than become what I don't want to be. With her, I stand in the woods and reach my hands to the sky and shout out, "I am alive!"

> *Go to the country - The muse is in the woods.*
>
> - Jean-Baptiste-Camille Corot *in a letter to Camille Pissarro*

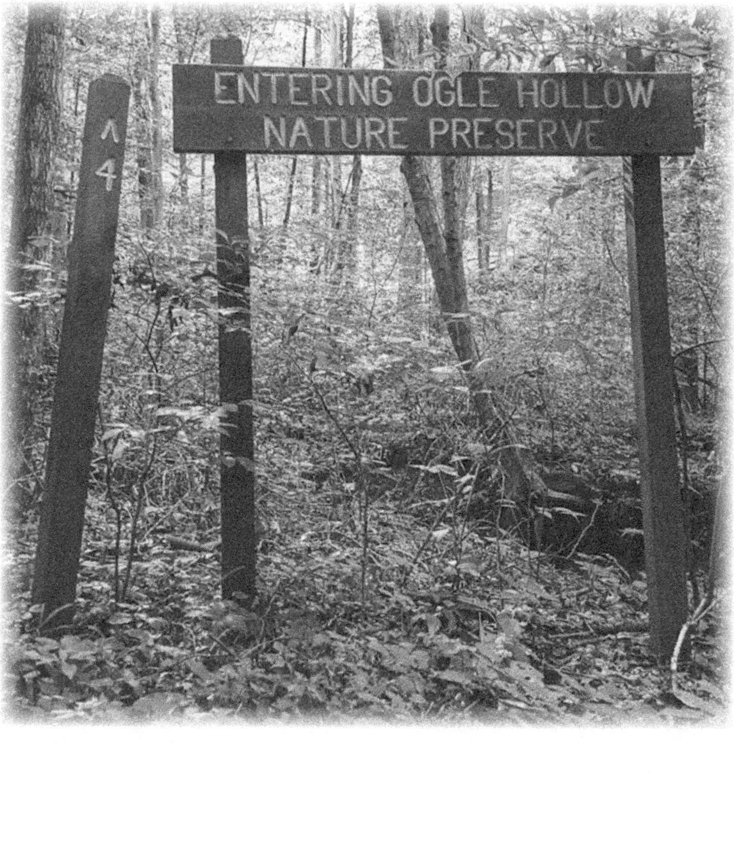
ENTERING OGLE HOLLOW
NATURE PRESERVE
4

A Letter to My Dad

June 20, 2018

Dear Dad,

I will forever look back on my childhood and my life and realize how wonderful it has been and how lucky I am that I have a father who cares so deeply about his children. That love and care has extended beyond my childhood and continues to this day. You are 90-years old now but I count each day you are with us as a blessing beyond measure. Knowing that through these years, you have always been here as a sounding board, a mentor, and most importantly as my father is a blessing. I have learned so much from the way you have carried yourself, each and every day.

A lot of the things I enjoy today, Dad, are the result of your encouragement. The first backpacking trip to the White Mountains put the exclamation point on what has been a lifetime of enjoyment in the outdoors. Those who know me would certainly agree; nature will always be an indelible part of me and balm for my soul. Your encouragement in scouting helped me achieve my Eagle rank, which to this day remains one of my proudest accomplishments.

Your commitment to your faith has provided me with a solid foundation. Your own involvement set a perfect example for me as I continue to be involved in the life of St. Paul's Episcopal Church. Sundays will forever have a deep meaning in my life. I have built my spiritual life upon your foundation.

My commitment to my family remains solid because of the lessons you taught. Even though you were running a business, there was always time for us. Our summer vacations with you and mom were epic and each brings back a wealth of great memories. Whether on vacation or at the end of a hard day at school, just knowing that you were always there provided a level of comfort that made growing up easier. Ken, Ann, Alice and I owe our tight bond to the lessons that you and mom taught.

You also taught me respect for all human beings. Regardless of origin or status, all are treated with dignity and respect. Your lessons stand in stark contrast to a world that seems more interested in tearing down than building up. You ran your business as if people mattered; it wasn't about profit and being first. You helped a lot of people make a good living and support their families. If one were to ask me of your legacy outside of family, I would simply say, he ran a business that cared about people.

I still remember a comment that was made during mom's funeral. A good friend said, with the deepest sincerity, that when he walked across the threshold of our house, he was always treated as family. You and mom set that example and I, too, know no stranger.

I could go on and on about the memories and examples of why you are a great father. I guess I could sum it up in one sentence; I give thanks each day that I have been blessed to be your son.

I Love You, Dad.

Dad passed away on November 26, 2018.

Dear Martin

I wrote this letter almost five years ago to my niece's husband, who lives in Vienna, Austria. I believe these words are perhaps more meaningful today than they were even then.

September 10, 2013
Columbus, Indiana

Dear Martin,

I hope this letter finds you and Kristen well, that your summer has been enjoyable and productive, and your fall season will be its equal. It struck me today that the art of letter writing appears to be lost so I have decided to take it upon myself to resurrect the art, or at least some reasonable facsimile. For the sake of expediency, I have decided to put my pen aside and use the keyboard instead. I am further setting aside the traditional means of letter writing by delivering this electronically rather than using envelope and postage stamp. I do so under the guise that rather than burning fossil fuels to run to the post office, I am preserving our natural resources by taking the easy way out. I have decided that you should be its recipient as it is a bit more difficult for you to tell me to my face that I am crazy or otherwise off my rocker, although I am looking forward to your next visit and the opportunity to have a beer together.

I was recently reading a collection of correspondence from Henry David Thoreau, the nineteenth century American author, and a few sentences to his sister on October 27, 1837, struck me as apropos. In it he wrote –

> "...letter writing too often degenerates into a communing of facts, & not of truths; of other men's deeds, & not our thoughts. What are the convulsions of a planet compared with the emotions of the soul? Or the rising of a thousand suns, if that is not enlightened by a ray?"

So at the risk of being philosophical, I have decided to share a few thoughts with you. Not a communing of the facts as Thoreau pointed out, although mine may not be truths in the broadest sense, even though they may feel like it to me. It is my hope that you will find a kernel of wisdom in the lines that follow and it will cause meaningful thoughts to rise up within you. These words are not meant in any way to provoke, in its sharpest sense, but instead to prod our thoughts to the surface while leading us to be more introspective about life on the planet and among humanity.

Recently, I read the following quote from Holmes Rolston III, a Professor of Philosophy at Colorado State University –

"Destroying species is like tearing pages out of an unread book, written in a language humans hardly know how to read, about the place where they live."

All of us, me included, have no concept of the number of species that are lost to extinction that we never knew even existed. This should be equally as sad to us as to hear of a known species that no longer exists. All too often these extinctions occur as a result of the impacts of humans on the habitat that we share together. As we continue down this path of destruction and more species are lost, when will the day come that we wake up and realize that we are destroying our own habitat and we may be next on the list for extinction? We do not live in a vacuum, able to go on our merry way, ignorant that our habits as individuals and as a species can have a negative or positive impact, be it right outside our back door or thousands of miles away. Our sun may burn out in a few billion years but continuing down the wrong path may make this event irrelevant to the human species. Just as one doesn't live in the same house with another person and not share a common bond, we are all bonded together as inhabitants of this planet - plant and animal. We should make every effort to keep the house clean, for there will be future owners.

Until next time, Martin, with love and regards,

John

The Old Well

*I went to the woods because I wished to live
deliberately, to front only the essential facts
of life, and see if I could not learn what it
had to teach, and not, when I came to die,
discover that I had not lived. I did not wish
to live what was not life, living is so dear;
nor did I wish to practise resignation,
unless it was quite necessary. I wanted to
live deep and suck out all the marrow of
life, to live so sturdily and Spartan-like as
to put to rout all that was not life, to cut a
broad swath and shave close, to drive life
into a corner, and reduce it to its lowest
terms.*

– Henry David Thoreau, *Walden*

The land that is now Brown County State Park was once the realm of the Delaware Indians, who hunted in the virgin woods that once dominated the area. The landscape looked quite different then, as the settlers and logging interests had not yet arrived. Beginning around 1840 and into the early 20th century, most of the park's forests were cleared for farming and logging, the larger trees at first for lumber and then the smaller ones for other uses. A walk through Ogle Hollow Nature Preserve provides some sense of what the land might have looked like before settlement and logging. Large trees, such as the rare yellowwood, sycamore, beech, and a variety of oaks dominate the canopy. The understory contains flowering dogwoods and redbud mixed with pawpaws, spicebush, ironwood, and musclewood. Ferns and wildflowers are scattered across the forest floor.

Many years ago, I came across an old well in the park. Not clearly visible unless you stumbled upon it, I found it after a blanket of snow had covered the ground. Lined with blocks of Mississippian sandstone, each more than 250 million years old, the walls were still intact and in good shape in spite of their age. There was still water visible in the bottom, although I would not attest to its potability. Just as the pyramids of Egypt were built by human hands, one stone at a time, this simple well was, also. The builder of the well may have thought that it had far more value than those distant monuments to the pharaohs.

I imagined a husband and wife, scratching out a homestead there by sweat and toil. The well is located near a small, intermittent stream that would have provided a good source of water in the winter and spring months. The area around the well would have made a nice site for a homestead, with ample hillside and flat ground for a few animals and crops. Other than the well, no human evidence remains. I can stand on a hill above the site and imagine a small farm, bustling with activity, smoke curling from the chimney, a meal being prepared in an outdoor kitchen.

Make no mistake, it was a rugged life. They would have

faced challenges we can hardly imagine today. Wolves, black bears, and panthers roamed the area. Hunger and diseases such as tuberculosis, typhoid fever, and pneumonia were constant shadows over this hardscrabble life. Although Nashville was only a few miles away, travel through the dense forests and over the rough terrain would have made the trip an arduous undertaking. Whatever crops could have been grown were likely supplemented by a hog and a few chickens, as well as a variety of wild game. History tells us that these farms eventually failed due to the poor quality of the soil, erosion, and deforestation.

By the early 1900s, our homesteaders had probably pulled up stakes and moved on, leaving behind a barren landscape. As the area was abandoned, the state began acquiring the land which eventually became Brown County State Park. With the help of the Civilian Conservation Corp in the 1930s, the forest once more reclaimed the land.

What led these former inhabitants into the woods to scratch out a living? Was it opportunity, the promise of a better life? Or, was it a desire for the solitude of the woods, to escape from more civilized society? In turn, what drove them away? Was it a future that never materialized, or the unforgiving land? Was it disease and hardship or the continued influx of people? We will never know the answer to these questions, for they have been lost to history.

When I think of these settlers and the old well, I am compelled to consider my own reasons for going to the woods. Why do I value so deeply the chance to spend time with nature? The answer is as varied and complex as each of the seasons. Whether during winter's icy blast, the birth of spring, summer's sun, or autumn's reflection, each of my experiences builds upon the last, forming a deep repository of memories, insights, and discovery. This is where I can escape for a while from the daily grind and explore my connection with the natural world. I can thumb my nose at society and become who I really am, free from the expectation that I conform to certain mores. My inner child is free to explore the wonders that surround me, every moment holding the potential to find something fresh or unobserved. I am as giddy as a schoolboy before recess. I cannot find or experience such during the day-to-day, where I often feel out of touch with the world. I grow homesick and driven to strap on my boots and return to the woods. The old well is the perfect metaphor for my relationship with the natural world: no matter how often I dip my imaginary ladle into its depths, I always come away refreshed.

A Letter to My Daughters

Dear Katie and Sarah,

It is truly a source of constant joy and my eternal privilege to be your father. As you continue on your journey to adulthood, I want to offer you a bit of advice. That's part of the joy of being a father; you have to at least hear what I have to say. You may ignore these words but here they are nonetheless. First, slow down and don't wish your childhood away, adulthood will arrive soon enough. I know you sometimes think it is pretty tough being a child but the expectations that are placed upon you now will pale in comparison to those as you become an adult. But fear not, for even now you are learning a valuable lesson that will help you beyond measure for the rest of your life.

What is that lesson? As you grow older, you will be tempted to suppress those things you did as a child, allowing the pressures of being a grown-up to become all consuming. Don't let this happen. You were born with and possess a sense of wonder at what you see around you. I'm not talking about the cacophony of electronic intrusions that desensitizes you to the wonders of the world; rather I am talking about nature, the natural world around you.

As you grow older, your childhood will likely fade into the background but I urge you not to let it go. Keep your sense of wonder alive, nurture your inner child, that part of you that continues to look at the natural world in wonder and cannot stop discovering something new and exciting. It is that part of you that is fascinated with what you discover outdoors, not indoors on the couch. It is finding the extraordinary in the ordinary; it is dropping to the ground to observe an insect, it is watching a chickadee flitting through the branches of a tree, watching the bees, planting a flower...

Rachel Carson in her essay, *"A Sense of Wonder"*, wrote,

"A child's world is fresh and new and beautiful, full of wonder and excitement. It is our misfortune that for most of us that clear-eyed vision, that true instinct for what is beautiful and awe-inspiring, is dimmed and even lost before we reach adulthood. If I had influence with the good fairy who is supposed to preside over the christening of all children, I should ask that her gift to each child in the world be a sense of wonder so indestructible that it would last throughout life, as an unfailing antidote against the boredom and disenchantment of later years, the sterile preoccupation with things that are artificial, the alienation from the sources of our strength."

I am not the good fairy, but Carson's words from 1956 are even truer today. Don't ever lose your sense of wonder at our natural world. Take the time to explore. Ignore adult expectations and do childish things. Stoke the fires of your inner child. Laugh in the face of convention. Ignore adult advice and free yourself, you have one life, live it like a child, and make the adults jealous. I feel for those that are so serious about getting a living that they lose their inner child and fail to see the beauty of life that abounds around them. They drive their new cars from their new houses and wander aimlessly to a place called the office. On their way there, they pass by the sunrise and sunset in pursuit of what might be rather than seeing what is.

So here are a few of tidbits to help you keep your inner child healthy as you grow and keep your eyes focused on all your sunrises and sunsets. Add to them, for this is the glory of the adventure called life.

Watch the sunrises and sunsets, always; climb a tree; watch a bumble bee; chase a butterfly and hold it in your hand; catch a frog; sing to a bird; watch a leaf flutter to the ground; catch a snowflake on your tongue; dance in the rain; go barefoot in the cool morning grass; observe an ant colony; lie on your back and watch the clouds float by; listen to the wind in the pine trees; smell a wildflower; rub your hand over the bark of a tree; sit in the woods and remain silent for a while; listen to the thunder; listen to a babbling brook; dig in the dirt with your bare hands; splash in a puddle; go for a walk in a snowstorm; make a snowman; wade in a creek; skip a stone; swing on a grapevine; observe a spider building its web; rescue an earthworm lying on the pavement after a rain; watch the tops of the trees sway in the wind; stare up at the stars and try to imagine where it all ends...

People may laugh at you and call you childish, but that's the point. Leave them be with all their adult hang-ups and expectations and be who you are constantly. As Ralph Waldo Emerson so aptly wrote,

"Insist on yourself; never imitate. Your own gift you can present every moment with the cumulative force of a whole life's cultivation; but of the adopted talent of another you have only an extemporaneous half possession. That which each can do best, none but his Maker can teach him."

My dearest Katie and Sarah, always remain true to yourselves; resist conformity; and keep your inner child healthy. Each of these things will nurture you for a long, long time.

With All My Love,
Dad

Source:
Carson, Rachel. *A Sense of Wonder.* Harper Collins, 1956.

The Artist in Each of Us

My grandfather lived a simple life. For him, it just wasn't a complicated affair. Don't get me wrong, he was not a simple man—he was a common man. He grew up one of six children in a log cabin on a farm in southern Bartholomew County. He spoke German before he knew English. He hauled gravel with his brother by horse and wagon to help build the state road near his boyhood home. He slept under the same wagon while hauling produce into Columbus on roads that looked more like dirt paths. He was confirmed (in German) at St. Peter Lutheran Church in Waymansville, Indiana in 1909, enlisted in the Army in 1918, and shipped off to France as part of the American Expeditionary Force in WWI. He returned home to the farm, married, worked a short spell for International Harvester in Indianapolis, and then returned to manage the feed store at the Farm Bureau Co-op in Columbus before retiring in 1958. After my grandmother passed away, he tried Florida for a season but reported that his idea of relaxation wasn't sitting on a park bench. He then settled into a very important role, Grandfather, which he performed above and beyond the call of duty until his death in September 1978.

I entered his life in 1959, and we became fast friends. He lived in a small bungalow on Cherry Street that still holds fond memories of Friday night sleepovers, CBS News with Walter Cronkite, pancake breakfasts, and the Major League Game of the Week with Curt Gowdy and Tony Kubek. I recall fishing trips, washing his 1973 Chevy Impala on the front lawn, planting tomatoes in his backyard garden, the hammock that invited me to lie on my back and stare at the clouds, popcorn and Cokes (in the small bottles), bologna sandwiches, Jackson County watermelons, and listening to Joe Nuxhall and Marty Brennaman broadcast Cincinnati Reds baseball on his Arvin transistor radio. The memories are so deeply carved into my soul that the weather of time will never be able to erase them.

This common man was also an artist. The hands that held the Heilige Bibel, a horse's reins, a plow handle, his Enfield rifle, the wheel of a tractor, or the hand of a loved one, also created beautiful, cane-bottom chairs. I am lucky enough to have two of his chairs, each woven more than fifty years ago. His fingers possessed some magic, for which, to paraphrase Copland, the common man deserved his share of fanfare.

The chairs, made of native woods, have intricate patterns woven into their seats, as taut now as the day they were created. I remember how he would soak the cane strips in an old metal wash tub and then work the cane in his hands to make it pliable. He carved his own caning pegs from a block of wood, using them to hold the cane in place as he threaded each strip through the holes of the seat as deftly as a dressmaker sewing a fine dress. Knowing how tightly to weave the cane was an art form in itself: too loose, and the seat would sag; too tight, and the cane could warp the chair bottom.

Those hands, oh those hands, weathered from years

of honest work, but still able to weave the intricate patterns in the seat of a simple chair. If he were alive today, I would hold those hands in mine and feel their history, the strength and passion he gave to his life, and what he ultimately gave to me. His may have been a common life, but it was one beyond measure. They say that the eyes are the windows to the soul—I say that the hands of the common man speak more truly.

My grandfather lived simply while he created art. I often ask myself if I have such talent. I don't weave cane, although I wish I would have taken the time to let him teach me. I don't paint or draw. I have no musical ability and I am not a sculptor. I do occasionally weave words together, in the hope that they resonate with someone out there.

My grandfather didn't sell his art; he did it for the love of his craft. I, in turn, share these words out of love for mine. I often sit in his chairs and when I do, I feel his embrace: the hands, arms, and soul of a common man, an artist.

Eulogy to a Friend

One of the greatest joys of my life stems from how two families, coming from different origins, became intertwined through the bonds of friendship. This story began forty-four years ago, when I met Horace for the first time.

I had gone to work for my dad as soon as I got my work permit, by his orders. Horace managed the print shop at Dad's engineering company and was the glue that held the building together—kind of a jack of all trades and, in his case, master of them all. Dad took me downstairs to the print shop, not quite by my ear, and introduced me to Horace by explaining that I would be helping him out that summer. As Horace later confided, his thoughts were *Oh, God. Not another kid to raise.* (My brother and sister had already passed through before me).

I was fifteen when I first met Horace and, being a teenager, I was full of myself. He was quite an imposing figure to a scrawny kid: a little taller than I, but barrel-chested with very large arms. I thought he was built like a brick wall. He had piercing blue eyes and an inviting smile. The wrinkles on his face—etched from a hard-scrabble life— belied his age. He would describe fights he had gotten into in his youth, and I would think to myself that I would have never wanted to have been in a scrape with him. He wasn't mean—just the opposite—but he was imposing.

Despite his misgivings about "raising" me, Horace and I became fast friends. Soon, I was going home with him for lunch, where his wife Sue would make grilled cheese sandwiches along with bowls of tomato soup, their infant daughter sitting with us as we broke bread. He would often take me home on the back of his Yamaha dirt bike, letting me wear his helmet. There were countless times he would stick my bike in the trunk of his car, so I didn't have to ride home in the dark.

I remember not giving one thought to the fact that Horace and I came from different socio-economic backgrounds. I simply remember that this was a man who, along with his wife, opened their arms to a bratty teenager who thought he owned the world. Their doorstep was my doorstep, their table my table. My mother and father treated Horace the same way. I silently learned that the things that bind us together are often bigger than we are, bigger than our egos. I cherish to this day a picture of Horace, taken while sitting at the piano in our living room in 1978, his harmonica in hand. He looks so at home at the ivories. I still have the memory of my 83-year-old grandfather sitting in the chair, listening to Horace's solo, enjoying every moment.

There were the fun times, the pranks, making fun out of work—and the "Oh, shit" moments: like the winter day I slid my '69 Camaro into the back of his old Chevy Impala. My ride didn't fare so well. Horace and I worked and played together, cutting firewood, playing softball, and noon runs. We sat in his living room, talking into the evening, sharing our faith, swapping stories, hopes, and dreams.

Once, Horace rescued me when I got in over my head putting gutters on my neighbor's house. There was the canoe trip on Isle Royale in 1994, an epic wilderness trip where the bonds of our friendship were further strengthened. I wrestled with his sons on his living room floor. Horace was also my rock when it came to questions about my spirituality.

Horace stood next to me when I married for the second time. I was there when he lost his father, his mother, and two brothers. When I lost my mother, he went on a long hike with me, giving me comfort with his words of consolation. There were our regular Friday lunches, usually at Steak and Shake or Arni's, and so much more.

He was a teacher to an upstart kid, counselor in youth and young adulthood, a stalwart friend through divorce and death, a spiritual guide and, quite simply, a friend beyond measure. He was always there, a lighthouse on the shore, an anchor in stormy seas. I can only hope I repaid the gifts he gave me, for it is too late to account for it all, to check the ledger. It is now left to memory, for death puts the finishing touch on all earthly things.

The world bade farewell to Horace today, taken from those who loved him before anyone was ready to part. This is my eulogy to my friend.

A Dear John Letter

If I could step back in time and hand myself a letter as I left Columbus North High School in June of 1977, diploma in hand, I would share the following thoughts with my younger self....

Dear John,

My friend, we have traveled together for a long time, never letting each other get too far ahead. We have been fellow travelers through childhood, school, teenage angst, young adulthood, and now into middle age. Whether being a husband, father, son, brother, or friend, we have stuck together through it all. Sometimes it feels like we have been playing a game of tag all these years, for youth runs from old age hoping never to be caught, and old age chases after youth always hoping to capture it. I owe you a lasting debt of gratitude that you have never really let me grow up. Left alone, I would have imprisoned myself in maturity, forever condemned to live a life of expectations, my success measured by how many cars I have, how big my house is, my job title, where my kids go to college, and on and on. Keeping my inner child alive and well has given me a wonderful outlook as I have traveled through this life.

I certainly received advice from many, but it's what I have done that matters most, not what anyone told me to do. Thoreau said (of those who would tell us how to live), "They have told me nothing, and probably cannot tell me anything to the purpose. Here is life, an experiment to a great extent untried by me; but it does not avail me that they have tried it." It has been my footsteps, the realities of my life, and where they have taken me that matters most, not the words of the so-called experts, for they are forever dispensing advice. The world is chock-full of those with the latest get-rich schemes, advice on how we can be better motivated to make a buck, or what we should do in order to lead the perfect life. If I had become addicted to all this advice, I would have spent more time indoors, devouring the latest volume instead of being out exploring the wonders of our world. It is the latter activity that has provided me more guidance than all the books in the self-help section.

I have reached the point in my life where I feel that spiritual fulfillment is more important than material gain. As I began my career and got into the habit of wanting more and more, I too often found myself feeling more like a shell than a sentient being. After I got off that roller coaster and focused more on the spiritual aspects of my life, I have received rewards well beyond those things bought with money. My spiritual exploration has taken me from Judeo-Christian values to the rich traditions of the East, such as Buddhism and Taoism. I have kept an open mind to the full breadth of all spiritual traditions, from wherever they originate, for each contributes in its own way to a better understanding of my inner being. Rest assured that I won't end my journey thinking I should have spent more time in the office.

The fearlessness of youth, that feeling of being immortal, abruptly gave way to the realities of age. It happened to me when I was thirty-three and underwent emergency surgery. I had marched through my younger years, daring whatever it was out there to come and get me, and it certainly did. I recovered and since then have tried to focus on my health and sanity, for these are the best gifts that I can give myself.

I have stayed very close to my family, for they are the roots that have allowed me to grow up with a firm anchor in this life's soil. From it I have nurtured myself and my own family. Death is the great unknown, but leaving this earth in the forest that is family is much better than the tree that withers and dies standing in the field alone. I have never forgotten the humble seed from which I sprouted, always believing that in the end, the humble will be exalted.

My parents taught me that to maintain an open mind and be accepting and loving of those around me, whether family, friends, or strangers, it was quite simply an expectation. Being a guide, a fellow wayfarer, and not a hindrance was my responsibility; humankind had enough struggles without the barriers I put in the way. My sojourn in this life has been much more enjoyable having embraced the human race, with all its warts and blemishes. Let me be clear that I am not perfect and I work hard each day to resist division and embrace inclusiveness. Being a true reflection of my parents is something I will always strive for.

There has always been a constant in my life, an anchor—something that keeps me grounded. For me, it is nature and seeking out opportunities to immerse myself in it. Whether gardening in my backyard or taking long hikes in the woods, I have sought out nature for its nurturing gifts throughout my life. It has kept me moored to the present, given me great memories, new discoveries, healed the wounds of life, and forever fed my inner child. If I were to lose this connection, it would be to lose my life.

One day not so long ago, I was presented with the opportunity to reinvent myself. When it arrived, I took hold and am riding that horse until I either break it or get thrown off. It woke me up from a Rip Van Winkle-esque existence and I am reminded that I truly possessed my future. It doesn't belong to anyone but me. I relish this ride like no other and am excited to see where it takes me.

Seeking out moments of solitude has always been one of my life's healthiest pursuits, and being alone in the woods is among the most refreshing. Being alone teaches me a lot about myself and, having spent enough time with me, I have actually discovered that I really do like me. It is in solitude that I have confronted the demons of my life, wrestled them to the ground, and left them behind to face life with renewed energy. As Thoreau said, "I find it wholesome to be alone the greater part of the time. To be in company, even with the best, is soon wearisome and dissipating. I love to be alone. I have never found the companion as companionable as solitude."

As I look back on my life, I know that things haven't turned out like I planned. I don't fret about it though, for I never had it all mapped out. My childhood dreams didn't turn out exactly as I imagined and there have been parts of my life that have come crashing down. But it's been okay, for change and adaptation are among the beauties of life. I have had grand experiences, like the birth of my four children, having a loving wife, the joy of family, pursuing my passion, discovering myself, and feeling the gentle touch of my spirit in each one. I have learned to roll with the happy times, the bumps and bruises, for I have had them all; it is what I have done with them that is important and not the events themselves.

So, my friend, this is not really advice but rather it is a reflection on a life so far lived. I think you would agree that it's been a great adventure so far. As we continue our travels through this life, will we stand firm with each other and take what comes? Will we be the tree in the forest that constantly reaches for the sun and is a haven to life? Will we dream as if we were just born and our life lies before us? Will we always pursue our dreams, our own path? Will we look at the world around us with a child's fascination? I will close with these wonderful words from Walt Whitman's, *Song of the Open Road*, for I somehow know we will always be side by side.

Camerado, I give you my hand!
I give you my love more precious than money,
I give you myself before preaching or law;
Will you give me yourself? will you come travel with me?
Shall we stick by each other as long as we live?

With My Undying Love,
John

Highway to Adventure

There is a stretch of highway in southern Indiana that, in my youth, carried me to a world of discovery. Although only about 18 of its 122 miles are in my home county, the adventures associated with this stretch of road are endless.

In my youth, State Road 58 began its westward journey at the county fairgrounds, south of Columbus. It made its way through a vast sea of corn, soybeans, and pastureland that seemed boundless to a young boy. Places like Ogilville, Mt. Healthy, and Waymansville lay along the way, small dots on the map but important waypoints on my journey. Waymansville, once a bustling German community, was home to many of my ancestors who now rest in the cemetery at St. Peter Lutheran Church. Finally, winding through a small valley, the highway climbed Dug Hill to places beyond my childhood experiences.

Many an escapade began at the county fair, which I often attended with my late grandfather. He was known to his friends as Alf, but to me he was "Gramps". Whether climbing on the farm machinery, walking through the livestock barns, eating slushies and cotton candy, or checking out the DNR fish and wildlife display, it was all a new world for me. These activities were of more interest to me than the midway, with its rides, games, and tattooed hawkers.

Grampa, a retired farmer and former manager of the feed store at the Farm Bureau Co-Op, was at home at the fair. He was my backstage pass to the agriculture show, put on by those who worked the land. These experiences instilled in me a deep respect for the traditions of agrarian life.

Farther down State Road 58, just south of Waymansville, lay Uncle Frank and Aunt Myrtle's farm. My aunt and uncle farmed 140 acres of ground and made a very decent living from the soil. This place was a young boy's delight. I would wade in the creek, catch crawdads, fish for bluegill in the pond, climb in the hayloft—pretending the bales were the tallest mountain in the world—and drink lemonade on the porch as I gazed out upon a vast sea of corn and soybeans. There were Bill and Silver, the old Percheron workhorses that my uncle once used to work the soil, and Daisy, the old Guernsey milk cow I would ride like a horse, along with the Hereford calves in the barn stalls. Trying to secretly ride them always ended in a good spill. One particular ride resulted in my landing in a pile of dung and then trying to explain to my uncle how the stains on my pants had come to be.

Aunt Myrtle was as much at home on the Allis-Chalmers tractor as Uncle Frank—the only difference being the large umbrella that provided her a bit of shade on a hot summer's day. I always thought that Uncle Frank deliberately chose the hottest day of the year to ask me to help put up hay. The bales were larger and heavier than I, and it often took four hands to throw them onto the wagon. I did my best, lest I get Frank's label of being "work-brittle", not a badge you wore with honor.

Theirs was also a life of faith, with St. Peter Lutheran Church at the center of their lives. Myrtle was the church organist. A trip to nearby Seymour usually meant that

Frank needed a new suit to wear on Sunday. My uncle's disdain for snakes was legendary, no doubt a product of his Biblical roots.

Each adventure would eventually come to an end and I would return home, rolling back down the state road with the windows of Gramps' '73 Impala open to the cool air of the summer evening. Often, I would fall asleep in the back seat, only to awaken as we pulled into the driveway. I would shuffle off to bed, confident that I had been a fearless explorer on that small farm south of Waymansville.

Oh, those summers past! Whether going to the fair, climbing in the hayloft, milking the cows, fishing in the pond, feeding the hogs, catching frogs, lighting sparklers on the 4th of July, or riding the tractor, each experience was part of a young boy's perfect summer day. Those days may be long past, but the memories that were forged remain an indelible part of me. My days at the fair and on the farm helped me develop a sense of adventure that I have held onto firmly throughout my life. Along the way, I learned some valuable lessons about faith, family, hard work, and our place in the natural world.

The Obituary

My dad passed away the Friday after Thanksgiving (the irony of Black Friday was not lost on me) and it fell upon me to write his obituary. No one twisted my arm, it was simply my duty to do so, a final gift to my father. It is the hardest writing I've ever had to do. The raw emotions of losing my father were laid bare with each word. How could I capture ninety years of a wonderful life in just a few paragraphs? I felt I had fallen woefully short.

The first sentence is always the hardest, the moment of death when the clock stops. *At 8:30 P.M. on November 25th, Kenneth L. DeLap passed away while an inpatient at Our Hospice of South Central Indiana.* I went on to write that he died peacefully, having lived into his ninetieth year. I continued with his military service, a few of his business accomplishments, and his community philanthropy. I then listed those who survived him and provided the final funeral arrangements. Done. Signed, sealed, and delivered to the newspaper.

What my effort did not impart were the love, emotions, and sweet memories he left behind. It didn't say that my brother, sisters, and I joined hands and said the Lord's Prayer with him on the night he died. It didn't say that I told him it was okay to die as the full moon rose above us.

It didn't say that we had watched dementia overtake his brilliant, soulful mind. It didn't tell of the unconditional love that he gave his family. God knows I needed his unconditional love more than once. It didn't say that after I prayed with him one night, he looked up at me with his bright blue eyes and told me that he loved my words. It didn't say that he gripped my hand strongly, one last time, with that grip he always taught me to give. It didn't say, that in spite of dementia, the last words he spoke to me before he lapsed into unawareness were, "I love you, John." It didn't say how I stroked his gray hair and kissed his forehead, one last kiss of love bestowed upon a father by his son. It didn't say that I held his hand as I felt the fire of his earthly life go out.

I had written the typical obituary, full of drab dishwatery words, failing to dig below the surface and mine the depth of this man's life. Who was he? What did he do that went beyond the ordinary? What kind of husband and father was he? What did he mean to those around him? This was a person who had touched so many people from all walks of life. How could the letters of the alphabet, arranged just so, describe his life? No level of elocution, no weaving of words, could ever do it justice. In his death, I will let the sweet memories write his epitaph.

Perpetuating himself by hammered stone wasn't my father's calling. He humbly gave of himself in so many ways and never expected nor wanted any accolades. His teaching was by example. The least of those around him was always better. He loved his brother, and that was everyone. He never cast the first stone, or any stone for that matter, because he recognized that he, too, was imperfect. He did not judge (too harshly) because he knew one day he would stand before the judge's throne. He did not complain about the fleck in his neighbor's eye, because he had a stone in his own. He showed his faith by his works and set a high bar for those around him.

Now the funeral is over, the last of the thank-you cards have been sent, and the obituary is safely tucked inside my grandfather's bible. To use a well-worn cliché, life goes on, though in so many ways, not like before. I have now embarked on a new journey, without my mother and father. I am a rolling stone, staring across a dark chasm into the unknown. But I know the lessons and the memories my parents provided will always illuminate the path, a beacon in the darkness. Writing his obituary, putting those painful words on paper, exposing the raw emotions of a father lost, marked the end of one life and the beginning of a new one.

III. SANCTUM SANCTORUM

Sanctum Sanctorum

Sanctum sanctorum is a Latin translation of the biblical term: "holy of holies" which generally refers in Latin texts to the holiest place of the tabernacle of ancient Israel and later the temples of Jerusalem but it also has some derivative use in application to imitations of the tabernacle in church architecture (Definitions.net).

The **Tabernacle**, according to the Hebrew Bible, was the portable dwelling place for the divine presence from the time of the Exodus from Egypt through the conquering of the land of Canaan (Definitions.net).

Years ago, a young boy bounded out of his house barefoot on a summer morning, full of wonder at the natural world around him—having discovered his sanctum sanctorum, he has yet to come back inside.

Often, I am asked how my love affair with nature began. That is a complicated question that still gives me pause. To me, nature is religious, it is scientific, and it is the past, the present, and the future. My passion for the natural world didn't emerge from a singular moment: there was no sudden epiphany. As romantic as it would be to say that one day, while walking in the woods, I saw an apparition that suddenly endowed me with the depth of love I have for nature, it would simply not be true. I think that, as much as I discovered nature, it has always been a part of me. It is in my DNA, a connection to my ancestors that stretches back eons.

Both my girls frequently go on hikes with me. Often, it includes a walk down the creek, throwing rocks whenever possible. The desire to throw rocks into the water is compulsory among children. Who hasn't skipped a stone or two? Being in the woods with a child teaches me to look at nature with wonder, as if I am experiencing it for the first time. I am *tabula rasa*. To view nature as a child is to see it without the prejudice that comes with age. I discard the "oh, I've seen that before" attitude and accept the reality that there are so many things that I can't explain away by scientific fact or religious dogma. It awakens the child in me to consider where the seeds of nature sprouted generations before. There is no greater experience than marveling with a child about the beauty of a walnut or picking up a stone from a creek bed and finding something unique about it. Perhaps it's letting a millipede crawl on your finger, or finding a tiny mushroom growing from a pine cone. Without slowing down, I risk missing these simple but beautiful things and the depth of the lessons they teach. I thank God every day for enabling me to view the world as a child.

When I go outside, it is really like going in. I see God in all nature, from the tiniest flower, to the sunrise, to the night sky at the end of the day. There is no other place where I experience His presence more than when I am in His sylvan cathedral. Let me dispel the notion that I am a pantheist, for I am not. I just see the divine in the things I experience outdoors. It is my personal belief in God that is one of the foundations of my natural being. My beliefs are not bound up in dogma, whether it is the Big Bang or Creation Theory. Don't get me wrong—these are all fascinating and relevant to various systems of belief and how we understand the world around us. Equally compelling to me are the creation stories of native cultures around the world, including those of our Native Americans. I don't take my direction from the pulpit or the laboratory. It wells up within me and is the product of my own faith and inquisitiveness. It is deeply personal. To me, if you get lost in the worlds of religion or science, you are missing the point. They are not mutually exclusive ideas—both can contribute to a rich and full understanding of our natural world. For me, when I step outside and look up into the sky, I have entered my *sanctum sanctorum* and my tabernacle that dwells within me.

Sounds

Discover harmony where it is most deeply concealed.

— Heraclitus

Unnatural noise, the ever-present hum of industrialized society, the sound of materialism, overcomes me like a plague. It wakes me up in the morning and it's the last thing I hear before I drift off to sleep. It wakes me up in the middle of the night. There is no escape.

In the early morning, I begin to hear the hum, and it builds. By the time I walk out the door, it is a full-blown cacophony of all the gadgetry and machinery of civilization. It follows me everywhere, the unnatural sounds fueled by the relentless pursuit of things. Sometimes, I think we create shit specifically designed to make noise. Even the things that are designed to soothe make unnatural sounds. Electronic waterfall sounds, really?

The cacophony of man-made noise invades the deepest recesses of my being. Whether it's the television, automobiles, airplanes, sirens, horns, people, trains, radios, toasters, microwaves—all serve as a man-made soup from hell. Even the damn toilet makes noise. My senses, filled with these sounds, often drive me to the brink of mental exhaustion. The noise compels me to seek out as much quiet as I can. It might be the relative quiet of my den after everyone has gone to bed, but more often, it's a walk in the woods.

I have fond recollections of my grandfather, a man of the soil who grew up on a farm. In 1895, the countryside of his youth was a different place. There was no mechanized machinery. The noise was the spoken word, the horse-drawn plow slicing through the earth, the cry of a baby, a hammer hitting a board, the sound of the crosscut saw, the handle on the well pump, the sound of Sunday worship, a breath. It isn't hard for me to imagine how noise has increased as the years have passed. Sadly, the natural sounds have been silenced or our ears have gone deaf. The sound of thunder, the wind in the pines, the rain falling, where have they gone? I wonder if I could hear such beautiful sounds in Shanghai or New York City, sometimes even outside my own back door?

When I walk in the woods, I try to walk silently, avoiding man-made sounds, careful about the spoken word, placing my feet softly on the earth. I am in God's cathedral, a place to be treated reverently. I am repaid by the gift of sound, the sound of nature. I hear God's whispers: the birds in the trees, the gray squirrels darting through the woods, the hoot of an owl, the sounds of the trees bending in the wind, the raindrops on dry leaves. His voice is in my ears.

Often, I can get caught up in the visual and forget the aural—but I am drawn back into the soundscape by something as subtle as the song of a chickadee. I think what it would be like to see this busy denizen of the woods but not hear its song. What if I were to see the rainfall but not hear it strike the ground? What if the wind were silent? What if I couldn't hear the buzz of a bee? I am truly blessed with all my senses and each connects me to nature.

I grow frustrated with man-made noise. Is there no end? Even a walk in the woods is punctuated by the sound of an airplane overhead, a car on the road, a barking dog. Sometimes, my headphones and the quiet of the den are my only escape. At least I get to choose the noise I want to hear. But, I go back into the woods to be with the natural sounds, away from the relentless desire of humans to possess the world. Is it a fruitless quest?

Homecoming

Every day is a journey, and the journey itself is home.

– Matsuo Bashō from *Narrow Road to the Interior* and other writings, Boston, 2000, p. 3 (Translation: Sam Hamill)

Homecoming, in the traditional sense, could mean returning home after an extended absence to reunite with my family. It sometimes reminds me of my high school days when our football team returned home early in the season. A king and queen were crowned, and they lorded over the student body—all of us full of testosterone and teenage bravado. Those years are long past and high school homecoming is now just something I read about in the newspaper. As I have grown older, I think of homecoming differently. It signifies many things now, each carved indelibly into my memory, no longer just a Friday night football game or walking through my front door.

It was a little over a year ago when I arrived at Indian River, Michigan and stared into the rest of my life. It was not a typical vacation: the world I had known had been upended in late June when I lost my job of twelve years.

To say the least, my life was in turmoil. On the last day of June, I walked out the back door of our rented cottage on Burt Lake, staked claim to a blue Adirondack chair, and gazed out at the lake. As I looked upon the calming waters, my mind drifted. I read Thoreau's *Walden* again, Li Po, Whitman and Wang Wei, losing myself in their timeless words. Later, I let the cool water of the lake wash over my body—a baptism washing away over a decade of sins. I thanked God I was there as I stared into my future.

Fast forward, and today I sit in the same blue Adirondack chair staring out at the same water. I recovered from the turmoil of a year ago and once again am leading a happy life—happier than I have been for a long, long, time. I have reaffirmed my resurrection in the cool waters of Burt Lake and now celebrate this place that gave me solace, vision, and guidance. This is a homecoming, taking its place in the hall of my memories.

A homecoming is something sacred to me. It is when I experience a crisis or disruption and then something happens that brings me back home to a place of peace. It is where I have been, what I have done—all the experiences of my life, great and small. It is the memories collected along the way; it is the good things. I have certainly experienced trials and tribulations, but I look upon them as making my homecomings that much sweeter. There are no do-overs for the things that have turned my life upside down, but I choose to let the good overwhelm them.

When I experience a homecoming, I know it, because I feel it inside: the warm embrace of an old memory. It speaks to me and says, "You were here once, and you are welcome back again." I then feel an ineffable joy that I have returned. It might be pulling an old book off the shelf, going for a hike in the woods, hearing an old song, tasting comfort food, sharing old stories with family, seeing an old friend, planting my garden, smelling a rhubarb pie in the oven, or visiting the graves of my ancestors. The people, places, thoughts, and things in my life have always been there, a constant reminder that I am on a wonderful trip full of memories, full of homecomings.

> *There are a thousand ways to kneel and kiss the ground; there are a thousand ways to go home again.*
>
> - Rumi

Fishing, Painting, and the Zone of Contemplation

We used to live on a lake, so I often took advantage of the winter freeze to do a little ice fishing. Just a short stroll out our back door and I was on the ice. I enjoyed the challenge of fishing in the dead of winter—all the more if the weather turned bitter. One winter, I was on the ice when our neighbor's fifteen-year-old son Edward approached and struck up a conversation. Edward was a rather contemplative soul for his age. Our exchange went something like this:

Edward: Whatcha doin'?
Me: Ice fishing.
Edward: Catchin' anything?
Me: No, not even a nibble yet.
Edward: That looks REALLY boring.
Me: It isn't really, Edward. I get to be outdoors, do a little fishing, and enjoy the weather.
Edward: Why do you like to be out in this? It's cold and windy.
Me: I don't mind the cold, and the wind possesses a certain spiritual element.

> Edward: If you're not catching anything, why don't you go inside where it's warm?
> Me: Why go inside? The fish may start biting and anyway, I'm catching thoughts before the wind carries them away.

I then got the, "You're a crazy old man" look. Edward shrugged his shoulders and walked back to his house. The wind continued to blow, and the fish didn't bite.

I've always considered fishing a contemplative pursuit. God knows I have had ample time to contemplate, since I usually catch more thoughts than fish. Anyway, grocery stores have seafood sections for a fisherman like me. I've caught more salmon, walleye, and steelhead trout at Kroger than I ever could in the wild.

I remember a fly-in fishing trip to Canada over twenty years ago. Joined by two good friends, we took off from our Base Camp west of Timmins and, after about thirty minutes, the floatplane landed near the only cabin on Forearm Lake in southeast Ontario. Taxiing up to the dock, the pilot dropped gear and fishermen off, quite unceremoniously as I recall, then taxied back out onto the lake. As the plane took off and faded in the distance, the feeling of isolation was quite palpable. The pilot wouldn't return for five days and walking out wasn't a viable option if things went to hell.

My buddies told me they would be making at least a thousand casts a day—it all sounded quite scientific. *Holy shit!* I thought. *There ain't no way this boy is doing that! A hundred casts a day and I'm done!*

I went for a lot of scenery and a little fishing, not vice versa. There were two boats and I kept one for myself so I could go in my own direction. It had one seat for solitude, two for company. (Side note: I caught more fish with my hundred casts than they did with their thousands. Of course, it had nothing to do with ability—it was just blind luck.)

We portaged between Forearm and Hardiman lakes to the east, where I spent more time holed up on an island, reading Thoreau, sipping on Jameson Irish Whiskey, and taking in my surroundings. There is nothing like contemplating life on a rocky island in the middle of a remote Canadian lake.

Fast forward to now. Our daughters are eight and twelve, and it has become apparent that separate bedrooms are necessary. My wife suggested that we paint one of the bedrooms for our youngest daughter. For me, painting is like being required to sit through a day-long corporate training session or doing our income taxes. I had left the corporate world, and I hired an accountant for the taxes—but I couldn't get out of painting.

I admire a person who can paint—houses, that is, and ceilings, walls, and trim work. I have met some painters whom I consider true artists. No Pablo, Vincent, or Claude here, just Larry, Leland, and Bruce. They can cut in a razor-sharp edge, roll on paint with nary a streak, and hardly a brushstroke shows on the trim. I am more the frustrated amateur who grows impatient with his lack of perfection. In other words, painting drives me nuts. There's no braving the elements, feeling the wind in my face, or just enjoying a beautiful fall day. Instead, I'm trapped inside, getting paint in all the wrong places, including my hair.

Nonetheless, familial duty called and I put on some old clothes and got down to work. The reasons I hate to paint came flooding over me. The adage "I'd rather sit around and watch paint dry," came to mind. If I go to hell, I'll be the Sisyphus of painting: condemned to paint the same room over and over again while the devil looks on with a dissatisfied smirk. As I painted, I nearly decided to go back to school and become a tax accountant, just for the excitement.

Time wore on with my brushes and rollers and a funny thing happened: as I got into the rhythm of my task, my mind became untethered and began to wander. I entered the "zone of contemplation", the same zone I enter when I am in the woods, or sitting over a hole in the ice, or relaxing on an island in a remote Canadian lake. Random thoughts coalesced into solid ideas. I even came up with this post.

Last night, my wife suggested that we paint our bedroom next, and I got that familiar feeling of dread. The thought of doing it all over again wasn't what I was hoping for. I would much rather be out in the woods, or at least sitting in the backyard, enjoying a beautiful October day. But, I will put on my old clothes again, pick up my paintbrush, and go off in search of my zone of contemplation. As I get paint in my hair, I might come up with another story.

Chased by the Sun

It was a beautiful Tuesday morning, so after I saw my daughters off to school, I headed for one of my favorite spots in southern Indiana. Passing through the covered bridge at the north entrance to Brown County State Park, I entered my sanctuary from the world, my *sanctum sanctorum*. I headed for Weed Patch Hill and Trail 10, or what I have always referred to as the Fire Tower Trail, as it begins behind that landmark. I put on my pack, silenced my cell phone, entered the woods and left my troubles behind for the rest of the morning.

For many years, I had let the sun chase me out of bed and into the office, but now I let it chase me into the woods. Here, I coax out thoughts about life and nature that I eventually shape into words. I no longer concern myself with how to survive in the for-profit world that too often treats a person as an expendable commodity.

When I was in the corporate world, there were some who would brag about how many hours they worked or how many miles they traveled on their latest business trip. They wore it like a badge of honor, won on the battlefield of business. What injuries did they sustain in their efforts? How many long hours, miles of asphalt, airport bars, or lonely hotel rooms was success worth? One day, they might find their fatted calf, but would they have the strength to celebrate?

The drive from my door to the park entrance is twenty-three miles, about thirty minutes travel time. I daresay I get more out of those miles than I ever got out of the thousands of miles I traveled during all those years chasing a dollar. What lies at the end of this trek? For starters, 16,000 acres of hills, ridges, and ravines in which to "lose" myself. There are the hardwood forests, spring wildflowers, Strahl and Ogle lakes, streams cascading down ravines in the spring, the howl of a coyote, the hoot of an owl, the fall colors, and the solitude of a winter hike. It's not the Tetons, but the park wears its beauty proudly. I have experienced each of its seasons and have found beauty in the smallest things. Whether hiking alone or with a kindred spirit, each experience is one of discovery.

It is more to me than just the scenery—this place gives me solace. It is my home ground, the place where my flesh and bones are rooted in the soil. It is a deeply spiritual place. When I am in these woods, the trees embrace me like family, the smells bring comfort like my mother's kitchen, the sights are like a homecoming after a long journey, and the sounds are like a favorite song. I have walked through these woods when I was full of both joy and sorrow, dealing with life and death. I have been here on a Christmas morning, a warm spring day, and on a cold winter night. I have broken bread here with friends and family. On this ground, I have celebrated my youth, welcomed middle age, and pondered over my remaining years. It is here that I feel more in the presence of God than in any church pew.

One day, I will take my last walk on this ground and embark on that final adventure, but my spirit, chased by the sun, will linger in this place.

True Books

Smaller than a breadbox, bigger than a TV remote, the average book fits into the human hand with a seductive nestling, a kiss of texture, whether of cloth, glazed jacket, or flexible paperback.

– John Updike

No, Updike was not referring to a cell phone or tablet. I don't suffer tablets well—or is it vice versa? More often than not, the first thing I have to do when I pick up my tablet is plug it into the charger. My daughter gets the most use out of it, connecting Netflix to the TV so she can watch Sponge Bob or Barbie. I got ambitious once and downloaded six electronic field guides on trees, birds, insects, wildflowers, butterflies, and mammals. The icons looked pretty on the screen, but that's about as far as it goes.

My cell phone is much the same. If it weren't for the camera and weather alerts, I wouldn't really need my smart phone, although it does make a good alarm clock. The smart phone is a conversation killer. I remember in college, when I went to class, there would be conversation among my classmates. My son now tells me there is virtual silence before class starts as students are bent over, banging out text messages, tweeting, or otherwise lost in the world of social media. I am convinced that there will soon be a new ailment directly attributable to bending over while staring down at a screen, some type of scoliosis of the neck. When I travel, I always try to do a quick count of the number of people who pull out an honest-to-goodness book in the airport or on the plane. I am certain, at least as far as my unscientific study goes, that I am in the minority.

I prefer to cling to that thing that's smaller than a breadbox and bigger than a TV remote: a paperback field guide, my well-worn copy of *Walden*, Leopold's *Sand County Almanac*, or Olson's *Reflections from the North Country*. Reading these classics on a tablet for me would be sacrilegious. There are those who say, "Oh, John, wake up to the twenty-first century." In response I say, "I have, but I am very happy having a foot back in the twentieth." I still like to hold the morning paper in hand, even if I have to wash the ink off after I'm finished reading. When I walk into my den or living room and pull a book from the shelf, I can feel the knowledge it contains. Each animal seems poised to jump off the page of a field guide; I plumb the depths of Walden Pond; the smell of the North Woods wafts from Olson's pages, and Sand County comes to life. I stare at a Kindle and see a black screen, void of that kiss of texture and seductive nestling in the palm of my hand, void of the connection I feel with each printed page. The pages turn...and the fire still burns (with thanks to *Goodnight Moon* by Margaret Wise Brown, illustrated by Clement Hurd).

To read well, that is, to read true books in
a true spirit, is a noble exercise...

\- Henry David Thoreau, *Walden*

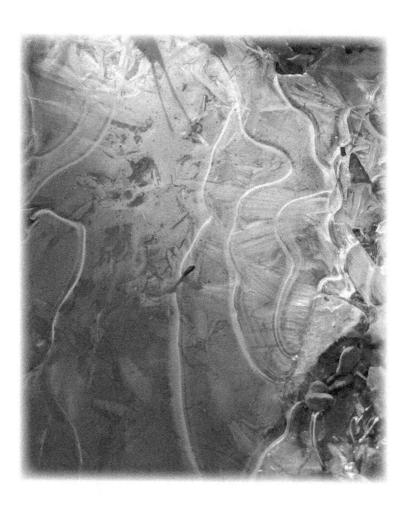

Why Nature Matters to Me

Okay, full-throated honesty: Winter is a rough time of the year for me, and the winter of 2017-2018 is no exception. Compounding the usual seasonal struggles is the fact that I am unemployed, wondering what lies ahead for me and my family. My depression is often profound; despair is the bogeyman who visits me often. My bed seems so comforting in the morning, but then becomes cloying. I awake and the house seems inviting, but then closes in around me. I want company, but then grow weary of it. I create distractions and try to force my mind to look to the future: I must, as the present can be a nightmare. But then, the future turns into its own nightmare.

I am confident that I will defeat this demon and persevere. Why am I confident of the outcome? I have nature, the companion of whom I have never grown weary. Through nature, I am able to process these emotions and derive a deeper, more spiritual meaning to my daily existence. When I let my mind and body escape to nature, whether a walk in the woods or a late-night stroll down snow-covered streets, I separate from the present and enter a realm most pleasing to body and soul; I enter the holiest of holies, my *sanctum sanctorum*. My mind soars above the earth: I am one with God and his creation. I strive for these moments, because they allow me to overcome the weight of my day-to-day struggles.

I went out last Sunday morning to Brown County State Park to worship with five fellow 'parishioners'. I didn't ask their faith; I simply asked if they could stand single-digit temperatures. All were in the appropriate dress for church: down coats, mittens, hats, and long underwear.

The woods were lovely with a fresh blanket of snow. We immediately saw signs of coyote: their tracks and scat were abundant. They must have attended early services; we were too late to hear their pre-dawn chorus.

The cold created beautiful ice formations on many of the remaining plant stems. We had started from the Nature Center, since the loop road down to Strahl Lake was closed due to the weather. We descended the short mile to Strahl Valley. A frozen expanse, the lake was covered by a beautiful white carpet. There was still some overflow and the spillway created a natural ice sculpture. The trees above the spillway were thick with rime ice created by the moisture rising from the creek below.

We wound our way around the lake and then back to the Nature Center, where we enjoyed watching the birds at the viewing station. Cardinals, nuthatches, chickadees, titmice, downy and hairy woodpeckers, doves and more entertained us. Sitting in the warmth, we all shared a feeling of satisfaction that we had braved the elements and spent this time together in the woods.

Every moment of that day reminded me that nature has my back.

My Leaning Tree

The game trail leading into the pine grove lets me know I am on the right path. I am greeted by the sound of the wind blowing through a large stand of white pines. My footsteps are silenced by the carpet of pine needles. I often stand in this grove and feel as if I am in a cathedral, hushed and silent except for the divine wind. Brambles act as sentries as I make my way through the woods. I soon cross a ravine where siltstones from the Mississippian age lie exposed. The sedimentary rocks at my feet were formed millions of years ago, when the area was a vast inland sea.

The small clearing I seek is not far from where I parked my vehicle, nor is it far from the nearest road. When I reach it, however, it feels like I am miles into the woods. It is here that I find my Leaning Tree.

The tree, a northern red oak, stands in a small clearing west of the Knobstone Escarpment in Brown County State Park. This species of oak is long-lived, and its acorns provide nourishment to a variety of wildlife. The clearing, sitting on high ground, was likely the site of an old homestead, or it may have been cleared by the Civilian Conservation Corp during the development of the park in the 1930s. Sometime in the past, an acorn sprouted on this spot and grew into the Leaning Tree.

Standing stately and erect, the Leaning Tree provides me with a place to rest. Leaning against its trunk, I stare off to the east and watch the sun rise above the woods as the clouds float by. A small pond nearby reflects the azure morning sky as tadpoles, water striders, and whirligig beetles go about their business. The clearing is carpeted with a variety of mosses and young bluestem grass; a tulip poplar stands in front of me and sassafras and cedar trees dot the clearing. A spring azure butterfly floats above the ground. Ants scurry along at my feet. Surrounded by deciduous woods on all sides, I feel as if I am anchored safely on this island amidst a vast sea of trees.

Here, I enter another time and place. I see my surroundings in more vivid detail. The fresh earth, decaying leaves, cedar trees, wildflowers—all give off their distinct aromas. In the early dawn hours, the birds awaken and their songs soon fill my ears with music. The blue jay, chickadee, titmouse, nuthatch, and crow add their voices to the dawn. The far-off call of a wild turkey, the howl of a coyote, the hoot of a great horned owl, and the wind through the trees add to this wonderful chorus. Even my coffee tastes better here. My senses are enriched in so many ways. Taste, touch, sound, smell, and sight carry me away on my sojourn from the man-made world.

The oak stands sturdy and strong. Its rough bark and gnarled branches are always a welcome sight. I have watched it sprout new growth in the spring and become full of leaves in the summer. I have seen its leaves turn red in fall and drop gracefully to the ground. I have heard the late fall winds whistle through its branches, soon giving way to the cold breath of winter. Through the cycles of time, it has remained sturdy and provided me a resting place during my sojourns.

In many ways, I am like the tree. For a little while, I take root here and let the rest of life hurtle on its way. I put the brakes on and take time to stop and listen. Time becomes inconsequential. I am able to contemplate things that are only flashes of thought during my daily grind. I count my own growth rings and think about those yet to come. This tree and clearing are gifts of nature, a cathedral of contemplation where the ground is my pew and the sky is the altar.

There is so much in this place: the flora, fauna, and tell-tale signs of geologic ages. It is also the place where the dust of the world is blown off my shoulders. My feet are planted on the ground, but my spirit soars to higher places. It is the character of this place, the rhythms of my life, and my coming and going that give it meaning. It is a place where I will always return, for I have taken root here. When I am away, I get homesick for my Leaning Tree.

The Solace of Water

*If there is magic on this planet, it is
contained in water.*

– Loren Eisley from *The Immense Journey*

A few years ago, I took my first trip to California and
the Pacific Ocean with my family. (It was actually
in 2011, which is maybe more than a few by most
counts, but when you get up in years you try to convince
yourself that the trip you took "way back when" was just
a few years ago. It slows the aging process).

It took me almost fifty-two years to reach the Pacific.
Lewis and Clark got there faster—and they didn't have the
luxury of planes, trains, or automobiles. It was still the
most sublime of moments to finally cast my gaze on the
Pacific. The feeling of awe was the same one I experience
whenever I am in the presence of any body of water.

I have always been drawn to the sights and sounds
of water. It is like a magnet, if only for a moment. I am a
frequent traveler on Lowell Road in Bartholomew County,
Indiana where it crosses the Driftwood River. I never fail
to cast a glance from the bridge where the river flows south
toward the town of Columbus. The Great Lakes have been

a part of my life since childhood—they never fail to attract me to their shores. There were backpacking trips into the Appalachian Mountains, when I was lulled to sleep in my tent by the sound of water cascading over granite boulders in a mountain stream. I treasure my moments on Isle Royale, sitting quietly and watching the waves crash on the rocky shoreline, imbibing a well-deserved whiskey after a hard day on the trail. Even a quiet stream in Brown County State Park has the same allure.

There is a deep peace that I find in the presence of water. I am quite content to pause a while and listen to the trickle of a small woodland creek, the rhythm of the waves on a beach, or the sound of a mountain stream. There is something more splendid about a sunset or sunrise over water. Even the wind-driven ripples on a lake or pond can be hypnotic. These bodies of water are like a songbird, their beauty to be beheld and their music savored.

While in California, we drove out to Point Reyes north of San Francisco, traveling across a remarkable landscape where broad vistas beckoned us as we made our way towards the coast. There were open expanses of wind-swept plains and rocky shoreline, trees bent by the relentless Pacific winds, and wildflowers waving in the spring bluster. We gazed upon the Pacific as it crashed into the rocks below Point Reyes Lighthouse; at South Point Reyes Beach, my daughter and I dipped our feet in the ocean. It was a baptism into the grandeur of this great ocean.

Awed by the Pacific, I was reminded of streams in Brown County, the Driftwood, the Great Lakes. Each body of water is a source of nourishment for my soul, solace from the hustle and bustle of twenty-first century life.

We are slow to realize water, -- the beauty and magic of it. It is interestingly strange to us forever. Immortal water, alive even in the superficies, restlessly heaving now and tossing me and my boat, and sparkling with life! I look around with a thrill on this bright fluctuating surface on which no man can walk, whereon is no trace of footstep.

– Henry David Thoreau, *Journals*

Morning Tea

There is no precise teatime for me, high, low, or whenever—it's the location that matters. I prefer my tea in a rustic setting, rather than with white linen tablecloths, doilies, fine china, buttered scones, and pinky fingers in the air. On a recent Tuesday morning, the woods of Brown County State Park beckoned me and I took the opportunity to prepare a little tea off the beaten path. There was no pretense, no linen, and no scones. I was the guest of an unassuming crowd of oak, beech, and maple trees, a pair of noisy blue jays, a couple of chickadees, and a gray squirrel.

Hiking is a contemplative undertaking for me, not a foot race. It's about the experience rather than the distance. I prefer to walk *in* the woods, not through them, taking the time to stop and observe the beauty around me. More often than not, I take the path that provides the most solitude. I find myself wanting to be alone more often. I'm not anti-social, but sometimes solitude takes precedence over society.

The path I chose to walk that morning was a long-abandoned road that led down to Strahl Lake. It beckoned me to explore its path through the forest. Grass-covered, with an occasional late-season wildflower, it was more a trail for white-tailed deer than people.

When I reached the lake, a light, wispy fog like soft cotton hung over the water. The water reflected the sky and the surrounding trees. I startled a raft of wood ducks that quickly took flight and disappeared into the morning—a brief but fulfilling encounter. Crossing the dam, I gazed down at the empty parking lot, smiled, and continued my walk.

Like the path I choose to walk, a spot for tea must also be carefully considered. It must have a level place for my stove, a comfortable place to sit and, more importantly, be secluded enough to be free from interruptions. I knew exactly where to go. I had discovered this spot back in March and had visited a number of times since. A little off the trail and up a narrow valley, it would meet my expectations perfectly.

My table that morning was a slab of Mississippian age sandstone, over 250 million years old, that was once at the bottom of a shallow, inland sea. It now rested below a small cascade in an ephemeral woodland stream. About four feet square and eight inches thick, it was covered with moss and adorned with oak and maple leaves—nature's linens and doilies. A smaller slab just above it served as my chair. Both were perfect furniture and the beautiful golden yellows and rich reds of the leaves the ideal canopy over my head.

I lit my stove upon this votive stone in praise of the moment. Briefly, I felt a little guilty. While the world was busy at work, I was in the woods, brewing my tea, sitting on an ancient stone rather than an office chair. My guilt drifted away as quickly as the steam floated off my teapot and disappeared into the morning air. I poured a cup and with my pocketknife cut a piece of dry salami, a little Welsh cheddar cheese, and a few slices of apple. Staring up at the colorful roof over my head, I broke bread and communed with myself.

I couldn't have dreamed of being elsewhere. Time seemed to stand still as I became totally absorbed in the moment. Soon, I would have to pack up and return to my truck. I knew, however, that it wouldn't be long before I would return for another sylvan teatime.

Sunday Mornings

*My profession is to be always on the alert
to find God in nature – to know his lurking
places.*

Henry David Thoreau, *Journals*

I've always been a spiritual person, believing stead-
fastly that there are things that science or rational
thought can't explain. I always stare up at the stars in
the night sky with wonder. I feel quite small and inconsequential. It gives me chills when I consider the small
place I occupy on this lonely planet, one among the bil-
lions of stars and who knows how many solar systems.
Sometimes, I allow my mind to travel to the far reaches
of the universe, trying to imagine where it all ends. I can
never imagine the end.

Although raised in the Judeo-Christian tradition, I
maintain a deep respect for a wide variety of religions.
I gain strength from the pantheon of religious beliefs,
each providing a new way for me to view my life, the
natural world, and impending death. If I were to close
my mind to those alternative beliefs, I would just as well
commit myself to spiritual starvation. I am always open

to discovering something new, a different way to reflect on my life and my place in the universe. I reject the simple narrow-mindedness that seems to dominate society. Throughout my journey, I have gained valuable insights from the full breadth of human spirituality. What a treasure trove I have discovered, because I took the time to unlock the chest.

Going to church was non-negotiable when I was growing up. A break was when I didn't have to get up for the eight o'clock service and could sleep in an extra hour—but Sunday school still started at nine, church at ten-fifteen. It was like clockwork, etched into my DNA. I remember coming home from college and staying out into the wee hours of Sunday morning. I would still have a buzz when Mom came upstairs, telling me to get my butt out of bed— no doubt with a mischievous smile on her face. I would crawl to the shower, praying for an early death. On more than one occasion I knelt at the altar, stared at the cup of communion wine and tried not to puke. Such an act probably would not have turned out well for me.

My upbringing didn't diminish my spirituality; rather, it planted a seed that still grows, a constant search for the truth, whatever that might be. As I've grown older, I have become more comfortable with the fact that I will never find the truth, but it's the journey that has more meaning than the discovery. Hell, I might not like the truth if I discovered it anyway. "Ignorance is bliss," they say. I have quit chasing truth down the rabbit hole, instead embracing the "stone soup" of my spiritual journey. There's a little bit of everything in it, but I'll never remember the recipe.

In my old age, I have become more relaxed about Sunday mornings. Church isn't as sacrosanct as it once was, and I often worship in the woods, alone or with chosen company. Nature is a religious experience, whether it's walking out my backdoor or off the trail. I find God in a lot of places, not just a church pew. It is in the woods, immersed in nature, where I am most likely to find God. From the tiniest mushroom to the broad sweep of a beautiful vista, I am reminded of the divine hand and all it has wrought.

This past Sunday morning, as the sun came up, I met my sons and brother in the parking lot at the local shopping center. We loaded into my truck and headed west on State Road 46 towards Brown County State Park. Entering the park, we headed towards our *sanctum sanctorum*, surrounded by the trees and beautiful fall colors.

As we walked among the trees, our service began. The prelude was the vibrant colors of the autumn leaves. We paused for prayer often, observing the leaves in their full dress, the flowing streams, the stray wildflowers, and the varieties of mushrooms. Chickadees, blue jays, and crows sang hymns as we breathed the incense emanating from the decaying leaves on the woodland floor. We tasted the wine that fermented on the wind as it carried the aroma of the woods into our mouths. We were in the presence of the Divine.

We took communion in a clearing, made coffee, broke bread together, and shared a little bit of salami and cheese. Not your normal elements, but holy nonetheless. A prayer of blessing wasn't necessary—God was with us. I didn't need to sit in a church pew; we simply walked into the woods and discovered Him.

Transitions

According to the *Old Farmer's Almanac*, spring will officially arrive on Wednesday, March 20th at exactly 5:58pm. The vernal equinox (also called the spring equinox or March equinox), is the point in time when the sun lies exactly above the equator and day and night are of equal length (or almost). The word *equinox* comes from the Latin words for "equal night"—*aequus* (equal) and *nox* (night).

I think of this as the astronomical rather than earthly spring. To me, spring has always been a transition rather than a line in the sand. I don't wake up one day and say, "Ahhh! Spring is here!" My spring won't come overnight or at 5:58pm on March 20th. I don't casually note the arrival of spring and then anxiously look forward to summer. Spring is something to be savored, as so many things that disappeared in the cold shock of winter come back to life. Spring appears before winter gives up its grip, and then sometimes refuses to let summer take over.

Although there is still snow on the ground as I write this, I have been seeing signs of spring for weeks now, not only during my walks in the woods but right outside my back door. Just yesterday, I heard the calls of sandhill cranes flying north over my house. I believe they have spring in tow as they head to their nesting grounds in the

Great Lakes region and Canada. The oldest crane fossil is estimated to be 2.5 million years old, so their song has been a herald of spring for quite a few seasons.

My perennial bed on the south side of my house has had daffodils poking out of the ground for weeks. They seem to know it's too soon to bloom, as the buds remain tightly wrapped in their bright green coats. The green is such a pleasant contrast to the snow that fell just a few days ago.

The mail also reminds me that spring is fast approaching: I have been receiving quite the collection of garden catalogs. The pages of these seasonal missives explode with color. Tomatoes with names like Brandywine, Mr. Stripey, Mortgage Lifter, Big Zac, Cherokee Purple, and Pink Wonder in bright reds, yellows, lemons, indigo and gold. My taste buds warm as I think about the fresh tomatoes that will grow in my garden in just a few months. No garden catalog would be complete without flowers. Zinnias in a variety of shades fill an entire page—the same for daylilies and hostas. Marigolds, nasturtiums, sunflowers, and a panoply of perennials bathe my eyes with spring hues.

One of my favorite birds is the northern cardinal. The male's bright feathers are such a pleasant sight against the snowy landscape. They seem to get chattier as spring approaches and they stake out their territory in preparation for the mating season. Their calls on a late-winter morning pierce the cold air and remind me that warmer weather is coming. It's like hearing an old song that I used to sing.

When I'm out in the woods, I like to turn over the leaf litter in late winter and search for the first sprouts. This late winter growth will soon become the first spring blooms. Spring beauties, harbinger-of-spring, violets, bloodroot and more will soon paint the woodland floor. There's a renewed softness in the air; the buds thicken on the tree branches.

There's no better reminder of spring's advent than a late-winter thunderstorm. We had such a storm in late February. My only regret was that it occurred during the day. I prefer the flash of lightning and the roll of thunder as I lie awake in bed at night. The crack of thunder in late winter is a pleasant alarm that goes off in my head, telling me to be on the lookout for spring.

None of these events relies on the sun lying exactly above the equator. They didn't depend on March 20th to tell them when to get started. They will happen on their own time, not because of some singular celestial event, but rather as a result of their own seasonal rhythms and earth's subtle signals.

I enjoy watching the approach of spring as it builds in a crescendo of life, born of the frigid days and nights of winter. Oh, there will be a snow or two yet, and a few morning frosts—winter's final, futile attempt to hang on. Meanwhile, I'll be keeping my eyes out for those subtle changes that are happening just outside my door and on my woodland hikes.

Sources:
The Old Farmer's Almanac at - https://www.almanac.com/content/first-day-spring-vernal-equinox

Cornell University Laboratory of Ornithology at - https://www.allaboutbirds.org/guide/Sandhill_Crane/overview

IV. FLORA
AND FAUNA

Let's Talk Turkey

Wild turkeys are making quite a comeback in these parts. Whenever I see a turkey, the wild kind that is, I often think of what I had once believed to be irrefutable: that Founding Father Benjamin Franklin had wanted the wild turkey to be our national symbol, instead of the bald eagle. *A turkey on the Great Seal?* What were the facts, exactly? In the midst of my search for the truth, I also learned quite a bit of new information about wild turkeys. I would have been among those who believed not only the Franklin story but also that one wild turkey was like another. I was wrong on both counts.

First, Franklin did not call for the wild turkey to be our national symbol. He simply expressed his appreciation of the wild turkey and his disdain for the bald eagle. In a letter to his daughter, he wrote, "For my own part I wish the Bald Eagle had not been chosen the Representative of our Country. He is a Bird of bad moral Character. He does not get his living honestly." The myth is further refuted in a few other online references, including The Franklin Institute's website.

Our majestic national bird eats garbage and carrion—so do the turkey vulture and common crow. The eagle isn't always the graceful hunter we picture it to be. I have seen it swoop down and pluck a fish from the water...and eat garbage at a dump. The hawk more closely mirrors the image of a graceful predator, perched on some lofty branch, eyeing its domain, before swooping down to sink its talons into its prey. But, let me say unequivocally though, I never tire of seeing an eagle: it is truly a beautiful bird.

Someone once asked me if wild turkeys can fly. You bet they can—up to fifty-five miles an hour. They can run at speeds up to twenty-five miles per hour. A flock blasting through the trees sounds a bit like a buzz-saw working its way through the understory. When I am out in the woods, I can tell where a flock has been foraging: it looks like someone threw a handful of grenades on the forest floor. This is not a dainty bird. It's not a chickadee flitting through the branches. That would be like comparing a B-52 to a paper airplane. The toms and hens can cut a rough path through the woodlands.

A second assumption I can refute is that one wild turkey is like another. There are in fact six subspecies of this bird on the North American continent! There are even wild turkeys in Hawaii, but they were introduced.

The six species on our continent inhabit different geographic regions. The eastern is most dominant, inhabiting the eastern half of North America from Minnesota south to Arkansas, then east to the Atlantic Ocean. The Florida or Osceola turkey inhabits, well, Florida. The Rio Grande subspecies can be found in Texas, Oklahoma, Kansas, and a few other western states. The Merriman's wild turkey is found in the mountainous regions of the west, with the Rocky Mountains considered its central hub. The Gould's subspecies is found in Arizona, New Mexico, and northern Mexico. Finally, the Ocellated is found on the Yucatan Peninsula and parts of Belize, and Guatemala.

I wonder what the Great Seal of the United States would look like if the turkey were emblazoned upon it, rather than the bald eagle? Would we be as awed? As a subscriber to *The New Yorker*, I came across the cover of the November 24, 1962 issue drawn by the late artist and illustrator Anatoly Kovarsky. His drawing depicted the turkey on the Great Seal of the United States. I thought it would be useful to compare Kovarsky's drawing with our actual national symbol. Check it out at https://diplomacy.state.gov/exhibits-programs/the-great-seal. You can view the New Yorker cover, along with an excellent online article about how our Great Seal came to pass at https://declaration.fas.harvard.edu/blog/turkey.

While you're there, you will learn that Moses, the Saxon chiefs Hengist and Horsa, and Hercules were once considered as possible symbols. Thomas Jefferson even proposed the nation's motto be, "Rebellion to Tyrants is Obedience to God." Hmmm. We know of course that *e pluribus unum* eventually won out: "Out of many, one."

Once you have had the chance to consider the turkey versus the eagle, do you think the Founding Fathers got it right? Are we scoundrels, or do we get a living honestly? Are we a country of eagles—or turkeys?

Sources:
Stamp, Jimmy. "American Myths: Benjamin Franklin's Turkey and the Presidential Seal," Smithsonian.com, January 25, 2013.

"Did Benjamin Franklin want the national bird to be the turkey?" (n.d.)Retrieved from https://www.fi.edu/benjamin-franklin/franklin-national-bird.

"Learn about the Wild Turkey Subspecies." (n.d.) Retrieved from https://www.nwtf.org/hunt/article/wild-turkey-subspecies

"Unsullied by Falsehood: Ben Franklin and the Turkey" (2016, November 21). Retrieved from https://declaration.fas.harvard.edu/blog/turkey

Scattered Bones

From the look of its teeth, the whitetail doe must not have been very old when it died. There was little decay and all the teeth were present. Its carcass was fully intact when I first found it in my in-laws'woods over two years ago. There was no visible sign of trauma, although I didn't turn the body over for a full inspection. I suspected that a hunter's bullet had found it and it eventually fell on this spot of ground.

All that remains of this once bounding creature is the skull, a femur, and a few vertebrae and ribs. What once was flesh and sinew is now only a few bones. Over the last two years, each trip back to the site has revealed a different stage of decay. Although sorry to see such a beautiful creature brought down in its prime, I have been able to witness how nature buries its dead.

Perhaps the first undertakers to arrive were coyotes, tearing open the carcass to get at the flesh and internal organs. Circling high overhead, the turkey vultures, using their keen eyesight and sense of smell, soon swooped in to join the feast. The ground turned up around the carcass indicated quite a wake of vultures. A murder of crows may have also joined in. Other diners were likely smaller rodents who gnawed on the exposed bones. Portions of the carcass were eventually dragged off and cached or consumed.

Even before the coyotes and vultures came, much smaller creatures discovered the body. The first were likely the blowflies, possibly arriving within minutes of death to deposit their eggs. Other flesh flies also soon appeared. Ants were likely at the carcass during the early stages—feeding both on the carcass flesh as well as the eggs and young larvae of the first arriving flies. A variety of beetles also came and went during the decomposition process. They included rove, carrion, hide, bone, and scarab beetles, to name a few.

The efficient work of all these undertakers was effective: for two years the deer had provided sustenance to a forest community, its flesh and bones sacrificed so that other species could live. As I glanced up from writing this short piece, I saw a vulture gliding across the sky, no doubt preparing once again to participate in the burial of another of nature's creatures.

Ophidiophobia

After a visit to the Brown County State Park Nature Center and a face-to-face meeting with the resident timber rattlesnake, I am compelled to ask: Do you suffer from ophidiophobia? After all, it is one of the ten most common phobias among humans. Walking through the woods in spring, summer, and early fall, I often keep a close eye on the ground. I am careful to watch the sunny side of logs as I step over them. I am also careful around rock outcroppings. Why so careful? I am watching for snakes and avoiding a chance encounter with these terrestrial inhabitants. Although I don't think of myself as ophidiophobic, I do prefer to see a snake before it sees me.

For many, the thought of a snake conjures up a primordial fear. Ophidiophobia—also commonly called herpetophobia—is an unhealthy fear of snakes. We don't have to look very far to see how this fear has been perpetuated through history. Adam and Eve accepted the apple from the serpent and suddenly understood the difference between good and evil. Medusa's head swam with snakes. The unbelieving Israelites were bitten by serpents in the wilderness. More recently, Hollywood brought us *Snakes on a Plane.* Throughout the religions and folklore of the world, the snake is treated as both good and evil. In spite of our phobias and religious beliefs, the snake plays a very important role in our natural environment, though we need to be careful around a few.

Indiana is home to four pit vipers or venomous snakes. Often referred to as "poisonous snakes", this is actually a misnomer. If a snake were poisonous, it would be deadly or otherwise detrimental to our health to eat one. In fact, I have found rattlesnake on more than one restaurant menu during my travels in the southwest. A venomous snake, on the other hand, is one that possesses a mechanism for delivering a neurotoxin into the bloodstream of its victim. These are the ones we need to be careful about, but not unnecessarily fear.

Of the nineteen species of venomous snakes found in the United States, the timber and massasauga rattle-snakes, the copperhead, and the western cottonmouth (also called a water moccasin) are all found in Indiana. They are referred to as pit vipers because they each contain a small, sensory pit below each eye that allows them to aim when striking warm-blooded prey.

Listed as an endangered species in Indiana, the timber rattlesnake is present in south central and southern Indiana in areas with heavily forested hills. Growing up to five feet long, this snake feeds on small mammals and birds. Brown County is home to one of the larger concentrations of these snakes. There have been a number of recent sightings in Brown County State Park and the nature center keeps a rescued timber rattlesnake on display.

The massasauga rattlesnake was once present throughout much of the state but is now found only in northern Indiana. It is often found in grasslands, marshes, fens or lake margins, dry prairie and hay or grain fields. It feeds on mammals, birds, and other snakes. Growing from nineteen to twenty-five inches long, it is also an endangered species in Indiana.

The western cottonmouth, rare in Indiana, has been confirmed in two isolated spots near Jasper in Dubois and Harrison counties. I often have people tell me that they have seen a cottonmouth in a local pond, lake, or river. Instead of a cottonmouth, they have likely seen a northern watersnake. This aquatic snake, growing up to fifty-three inches long, feeds primarily on fish, but it will also eat other snakes, amphibians, and small mammals. It can be quite aggressive if disturbed. If you see a snake that you think might be a cottonmouth, pay close attention to the shape of the head. The cottonmouth has the classic, diamond-shaped head of the pit viper while the northern watersnake has a more oblong head. Another differentiator is the swimming posture of each snake. The northern watersnake will swim with just its head and neck above the surface, while the entire body of the cottonmouth appears to float on top of the water.

The last species of pit viper found in Indiana is the northern copperhead. Of all the pit vipers, this is the species we are most likely to encounter. It is found in the Ohio River Valley and north to Franklin County in the east and Fountain and Vermillion counties to the west. Typically spotted in hilly and rocky areas, they grow to three feet long and feed mainly on small rodents and insects.

I encourage you to do more research about our native pit vipers. You can check out a few of the field guides and references I use in the Field Guide and Reference Library of my website. Instead of letting ophidiophobia overcome you, gain some understanding of these secretive reptiles and become familiar with their habits and habitats. Respect them for the contribution they make to our natural environment and gain some healthy respect for their space in the outdoors.

Source:

Minton, Jr., Sherman A. *Amphibians and Reptiles of Indiana*, Indiana Academy of Sciences, 2001.

I Once Met Chuck Will's Widow

Chuck Will was a stranger to me. Our paths had never crossed, and I can honestly say that I was not aware he had a widow. Oddly enough, I know of another Chuck Will, but he is not the subject of this writing. This is about Chuck's widow and not about either Chuck.

I crossed paths with Chuck's widow this past Memorial Day weekend while my family and I were in the Red River Gorge in Eastern Kentucky. The Gorge, located within the Daniel Boone National Forest, abounds with natural stone arches, unusual rock formations, and beautiful sandstone cliffs. It is a wonderful place for hiking and rock climbing, if you're the daring type. It is also a nice place to just get away, to blow the dust of the world off your shoulders and find an inner peace.

Fighting our way through rush hour and holiday traffic in Louisville and Lexington was not exactly finding our inner peace, but we finally made our way onto the Bert T. Combs Mountain Parkway on the sunrise side of Lexington. As you drive east on the parkway, you are reminded that you are entering a different world. The bluegrass horse farms of Lexington give way to the mountains, hills and hollers of eastern Kentucky, the Appalachians.

Passing by Clay City, Waltersville, and Stanton, we left the parkway at Slade and headed south on Highway

11. The road curved alongside sandstone cliffs and rocky streams. I felt like I was in another country, much farther away from home than a mere three hours. Past Zachariah, just past Zoe, we turned off 11 at the local VFW lodge. Descending a gravel road past a small cemetery, we entered a dense wood of oak and maple, with mountain laurel in full bloom. Away from the hustle and bustle of our other world, we had arrived at our destination, aptly named The Retreat. Little did I suspect an encounter with Chuck Will's Widow.

With a little more daylight ahead of us, we opted for assistance with our evening meal and headed for Hill Top Pizza, which advertised subs, salads, and hot wings. Let me just say that the pizza and dry-rubbed hot wings were palate-pleasers. I didn't try the salad, but I did get to know the resident feline. She was helping herself to a bit of pizza when I left. Hill Top was a local joint that helped us get into the rhythm of the local scene.

After a good meal, we settled into the peace and tranquility of our retreat. As the day began to turn and the sun dipped below the horizon, the sounds of night soon chased the day away. The crickets sang, the frogs croaked, and an occasional owl hooted. I was enjoying a nice Kentucky moonlight stroll when a strange sound broke the night air. In the dark stillness, my ears strained to hear what my eyes could not see. It came from deep in the woods, but the sound was as clear as if someone were whispering in my ear. Was it a ghost from the cemetery up the hill, or was someone lost in the woods? I listened intently, my sense of hearing more acute as my sight was limited.

It kept calling, and the voice became clearer: *chuck-wills-widow, chuck-wills-widow!* It would stop for just a moment and then call again, *chuck-wills-widow, chuck-wills-widow!* My imagination got the better of me for a moment and I thought I heard: *"I am Chuck Will's Widow, I am Chuck Will's Widow!"*

Before the chill of fear overcame me, I remembered reading about this call in one of my bird guides. I was being granted the rare opportunity to hear the call of Chuck Will's Widow, a member of the nightjar family of birds. This bird, a denizen of the night, is rarely seen during the day, so the opportunity to listen to its distinctive nocturnal song was a special gift. As I listened to the calls, my imagination ran wild in the darkness and I began to wonder if it really might be Chuck Will's Widow, calling out to those who would listen. Perhaps her body is buried in the small cemetery up the hill, while her spirit wanders lost in these Kentucky hills. She may be looking for a home, a place where her spirit can find peace. Instead, could she be cursed to wander through these woods for eternity, calling *"I am Chuck Will's Widow, I am Chuck Will's Widow?"*

My goosebumps grew a bit: it was time to go inside.

Source:
Peterson, Roger Tory. *Field Guide to Birds of North America*, Peterson Field Guides, Houghton Mifflin, 2008

Muscles or Mussels

I s heelsplitter the name of a muscle in your foot—or is it a mussel? How about triceps, wartyback, deltoids, monkeyface, biceps, pocketbook, quadriceps, papershell, tibialis, pigtoe, gluteus maximus, sheepnose, sartorius, catspaw, trapezius, lilliput, soleus, or mucket? Can you pick the mussels from the muscles?

Chances are you might be more familiar with the names of your muscles versus those of freshwater mussels. Don't be disappointed if you don't know much about mussels. They spend their lives partially or totally submerged in permanent bodies of water. The vast majority are found in streams, while some are found in ponds or lakes.

So, what is a mussel? Mussels are bi-valve mollusks with elongated shells and are cousins to the squid, octopus, nautilus, snail, and slug. They are an important source of food for fish, raccoons, muskrats, otters, turtles, and waterfowl. Some may refer to the generic term "clam" when they find a shell on the river bank or happen across a live mussel. Although both are bi-valve mollusks, the clam and mussel are of different species: a clam is not a mussel and a mussel is not a clam.

A mussel possesses an incurrent siphon and an excurrent siphon. To obtain food, it draws water through the incurrent siphon, where it filters out microscopic plant and animal material suspended in the water. Waste is then discharged through the excurrent siphon.

Most freshwater mussel species are of separate sexes. The male releases sperm into the water, which enters the female through the incurrent siphon where the eggs are fertilized. The fertilized eggs develop into an intermediate larval stage (glochidia) and are stored in the female's gills. In spring or summer, the glochidia are expelled and seek out a host to parasitize. Depending on the species of mussel, the glochidia are either internal parasites or external parasites. The host is usually a fish and the glochidia form cysts on either the gills or fins of their host.

While in the cyst, the glochidia change form and begin to resemble mussels. They then break free of the cyst and drop to the stream or lake bottom to begin independent lives. The period of attachment lasts from one to twenty-five weeks, depending on a variety of factors including the host, location of attachment, and water temperature. Mussels are long-lived, with some reported to have survived over a hundred years.

Unfortunately, many mussels are endangered and others have been extirpated. According to the 2010 *Wildlife Diversity Report* published by the Indiana Department of Natural Resources, freshwater mussels are the most endangered group of animals in Indiana. Historically, seventy-seven species were found in the state. Of these, nineteen are completely gone or no longer producing. Currently, there are twenty-four species in Indiana listed as state- or federally-endangered or of special concern.

Threats to the state's mussel population include overharvesting, pesticides, herbicides and other chemicals, run-off, siltation, poor land management practices, and competition from exotic species such as the zebra mussel. Quite a number of foes are arrayed against our mussels.

Let's put our muscles to work and protect our mussels. Support clean-up efforts, wise land management practices, and protection of our streams and lakes.

Here are a few more of the common names of our freshwater muscles:

Spectacle case • Washboard • Pistolgrip • Winged Mapleleaf • Rabbits Foot • Fatmucket Pimpleback • Threeridge • Wabash Pig-toe • Ebonyshell • Rayed bean • Elephant-ear Spike • Pondhorn Floater • Elktoe • Rock-pocketbook • Kidneyshell • Bleufer • Fanshell Purple wartyback • Butterfly • Hickorynut • Deertoe • Fawnsfoot • Fat Pocketbook Higgins eye • Snuffbox • Ring Pink • Pyramid pigtoe • Rainbow • Creeper • PeeWee

Source:
Cummings, Kevin S. and Christine A. Mayer, *Field Guide to Freshwater Mussels of the Midwest*, Illinois Natural History Survey, 1992.

A Kettle of Vultures

Y ou see them soaring with broad, dark wings on the thermals rising above the earth, circling as as they search for carrion. Probably characterized more than any other bird species, they have appeared in many cartoons and comic strips, such as Gary Larson's *The Far Side*. I am talking about the turkey vulture (*Cathartes aura*) or the black vulture (*Coragyps atratus*) as they are commonly called, "buzzards".

This turkey vulture won't be winning any beauty contests: its head has no feathers, just wrinkled skin. All the better for it to stick its head inside a carcass and pluck out a tasty morsel—no sense getting one's "hair" messed up while eating.

I have seen the turkey vulture in a number of settings. Needless to say, it is a very adaptable bird. I recently passed two, feeding on a road-kill squirrel on a rural county road. I have seen them in farm fields: large numbers perched on power line stanchions, and more recently on the roof of a local church.

Despite their lack of beauty, vultures really do serve a valuable purpose. They are the dog under nature's dining room table. They clean up what is left on the road or in the field. Recently, while hiking in Brown County, I found the remains of a deer carcass just off the trail. The bones were stripped clean, no doubt a result of the "vulture dance".

One of only two avian scavengers in the eastern United States, the turkey vulture is from twenty-six to twenty-seven inches long with a maximum wingspan of six feet. Up close, the small, bald red head gives the adult bird away. The head of the immature turkey vulture is blackish in color. Note the two-toned wings when looking up at this bird as it soars in search of its next meal. The turkey vulture is present throughout the United States, southern Canada, and Mexico. It can be found year-round in parts of southern Indiana and migrates as far south as Mexico in winter.

In southern Indiana, the turkey vulture's territory overlaps with that of the black vulture. Initially difficult to differentiate, the black vulture is smaller in size, black in color and with a gray head in adults. Also, when seen from below, the black vulture has a whitish patch towards its wingtip.

Possessing a keen sense of smell, the turkey vulture can detect dead and decaying animals even in wooded settings. They feed exclusively on carrion from as small as a mouse to as large as a deer. It may be the increase in the white-tail deer population that has led to the rising population of turkey vultures. More deer means more road-kill and, consequently, more carrion. They are site-feeders and regurgitate food later for their young. Because they feed on carrion, their feet and talons are small and weak.

The turkey vulture lays its eggs in remote areas generally inaccessible to predators. This may include cliffs, hollow logs, caves, or dense shrubbery. The female typically lays two eggs. There is little or no nest, with the eggs often laid on bare ground. The young are carefully concealed to avoid predators.

The turkey vulture may not be the most beautiful bird in Indiana, but it may be one of the most useful. Keep your eyes peeled, to the sky. Searching from above for food, vultures wait for mother nature to drop a morsel from the dinner table. You can be sure they will be ready to snatch it up.

Source:

Clark, William S. and Brian K. Wheeler, *Hawks of North America*, Peterson Field Guides, Houghton Mifflin, 2001.

Small is Beautiful

*In every walk with nature one receives
more than he seeks.*

- John Muir, *Travels in Alaska*

O kay, so like many, I love a grand vista. The view
from the top of a mountain takes my breath away.
I remember reaching the top of Mt. Marcy in the
Adirondacks and catching a view before the clouds socked
us in. I think back to the sunrise I saw over the Atlantic
Ocean from the top of Mt. Washington in the White
Mountains of New Hampshire. Watching the mountain
casting its shadow to the west over Vermont made me
feel quite insignificant. A sunset over the hills of Brown
County, Indiana can be awe-inspiring. I am equally
taken in by Ansel Adams' majestic photographs taken
in Yosemite. The sweeping bend of the Ohio River near
Leavenworth, Indiana makes a fine backdrop for a good
meal at the Overlook Restaurant.

Equally inspiring to me are the small things in nature—those things that lie close at hand. It takes a keen
eye to spy them, but there is so much to be discovered
close to the ground. By keeping my eye peeled I have

discovered the unique bark on a beech tree; the smallest of mushrooms poking up through the leaf litter; an eastern box turtle lumbering on its way; the unique colors and shapes of the fall leaves that lay strewn across the ground; frost flowers; oak galls; bumble bees and butterflies on my garden flowers; a katydid on my daughter's hand; a lizard hiding on the bark of a pine tree: all gifts from nature.

In *Walden*, Henry David Thoreau wrote, "Direct your right eye inward, and you will find a thousand regions in your mind yet undiscovered/ Travel them, and be expert in home cosmography." I say also, look down and around you and you will truly see that small is beautiful and there are thousands of things before you yet undiscovered.

There are always flowers for those who want to see them.

- Henri Matisse, from *Flam, Jack, Matisse on Art*, University of California Press, 1995

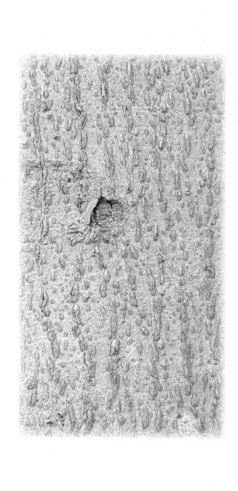

The Ohi:yó

The Seneca call it the *Ohi:yó*, the "Good River", and the Shawnee call it the *pelewa thiipi*. The early French explorers called it *la Belle Rivière*, the "Beautiful River". Prior to shipping out to France in 1918, my grandfather did his army basic training at Camp Taylor in Louisville. Seeing the Ohio River for the first time, he referred to it as "Big Waters" in a letter home. It must have been quite a sight for him, since White Creek was probably the biggest waters he had ever seen.

As "big waters" go, the Ohio River dominates the geography of southern Indiana. Stretching along Indiana's southern border, the river has long controlled the rhythm of life along its banks. The history of our nation is intertwined with the river, with historical figures like Meriwether Lewis, William Clark, Daniel Boone, Abraham Lincoln, and countless others etching their names in its currents. But the river is more than just the people or the events that have been swept up in the flow of history. Long before there were towns and people, the river carved its place in the geological history of the states in the Ohio River Valley. Ancient events shaped the land and the people who came thousands of years later.

The Ohio River begins its journey at the confluence of the Allegheny and Monongahela Rivers at Pittsburgh.

As it meanders westward, it passes by bustling cities like Cincinnati and Louisville, and quiet river towns such as Rising Sun and Metropolis, before ending its journey at Cairo, Illinois. Before the river was dammed to allow for boat traffic, it was relatively shallow, with depths of three to twenty feet. In some places, one could even walk across the river.

The geologic history of the Ohio is tied up in the pre-historic Teays River and multiple glacial periods that occurred during the Pleistocene Epoch. Prior to the formation of the river we know today, much of the east-central United States was drained by the ancient Teays River system. Originating over two million years ago in the Tertiary Period in what is now North Carolina, it flowed north through present-day Virginia, West Virginia, and Ohio before turning westward and continuing on through northern Indiana and Illinois. It eventually drained into an embayment of the Gulf of Mexico, now occupied by the Mississippi River. Much of the Teays River Valley, up to two miles wide in places, is now buried under glacial sediment as deep as five hundred feet.

One of the earliest glacial periods of the Pleistocene dammed the northward flow of the Teays and created a vast lake, rising to an elevation of nearly nine hundred feet and covering an estimated 7,000 square miles in southern Ohio, Kentucky and West Virginia. Eventually, the water of this lake breached its drainage divides and created new drainage patterns. This breach marked the birth of the modern Ohio River drainage system. The cycles of damming and overflowing continued during subsequent glacial periods that pressed farther south. Most notably, the Wisconsin Glacier gradually changed the river's path to what we see today.

The Ice Age is one of those periods in geologic history that fascinates me due to its enormity. With temperatures too cold for the snow to melt off, the accumulation eventually created the glaciers that slowly pushed into the Ohio Valley. I can imagine staring at a wall of ice over a mile high, with constant winds and a landscape as desolate as the dark side of the moon. One can be sure that any living thing would have had a rough time of it, which makes me think that a repeat would not go well for humankind.

The Ohio, although beautiful along many of its more rural stretches, is very different from the one of history. Drastically changed since the construction of the lock and dam systems, there is very little that looks like the river on which the Shawnee and Seneca paddled just a few hundred years ago. Humans have made our mark on the river, some good and some bad, but be assured the Ohi:yó will continue on, following its own rhythm and not ours.

Sources:

The Teays River, GeoFacts No. 10, Ohio Department of Natural Resources, Division of Geological Survey, November 1995.

Fleming, Anthony. *Ice Age in Indiana*, Indiana Geological & Water Survey. You can access this paper at https://igws.indiana.edu/Surficial/IceAge

The American Beech

I frequently tramped eight or ten miles through the deepest snow to keep an appointment with a beech-tree, or a yellow birch, or an old acquaintance among the pines.

- Henry David Thoreau, *Walden*

The first thing I learned about trees as a child was that they were supposed to be climbed. If I saw a low-hanging branch, up I would go. Whether it was the sugar maple in our backyard on Elm Street, the sweet gum on Chestnut Street, or the old apple trees on my uncle's farm, I viewed all trees as things to be scaled. With age, heights have lost their appeal and I now prefer to view trees from solid ground. No longer do I consider them something to be conquered; rather, I see them for their individual and collective beauty.

Although I love a stand of pines, I am especially drawn to the hardwoods: beeches, oaks, maples, hickories, cherries and more. Spending time in the woods among our native hardwood trees has been one of the blessings of my life. To walk among the trees throughout the four seasons has allowed me to truly appreciate the cycle of life in the woods. It has provided me with a deeper appreciation that life is change, but also with the belief that there will always be a spring.

Of our native hardwoods, the American beech is one of my favorites. An oil painting of a stand of beeches hangs above my fireplace, painted in the 1940s by the Hoosier artist Bryan Tarlton. His brushstrokes bring to life the gray bark of the trees, the leaves still clinging to the branches, a small woodland pond, and the bold clouds of a fall sky. The painting invites me to step into it and go for a ramble in its woods. The first verse of the poem, "Beechwoods at Knole", by Victoria Sackville West comes to mind:

> How do I love you, beech-trees, in the autumn,
>   Your stone-grey columns a cathedral knave
> Processional above the earth's brown glory!

The American beech stands straight and tall, its smooth, gray bark gleaming in the sun as its boles extend out from the trunk to grasp the earth. It invites me to reach out and touch it, to feel its skin. Its pale-yellow leaves hang on into winter, providing a stark contrast to the browns and grays that color the woods. When a brisk wind blows, the leaves dance on the branches and their rustling sings a haunting ode to winter. Yet, when I look at these trees standing boldly in the woods, I am reminded that last year's leaves will soon fall away, and spring will once again return.

> *God is the experience of looking at a tree*
> *and saying, "Ah!"*

> \- Joseph Campbell, *The Power of Myth*

Source:
Jackson, Marion T. *101 Trees of Indiana*. Indiana University Press, 2004.

Peattie, Donald Cutross. *A Natural History of North American Trees*. Trinity University, 2013.

Sly as a Fox

"Sly as a fox", the "fox in the henhouse", "crazy like a fox" are a few of the clichés concerning one of our familiar omnivores. Two species of fox occur in Indiana, the gray (*Urocyon cinereoargenteus*) and the red (*Vulpes vulpes*). The red fox is more abundant than the gray and owes much of its territorial expansion to man. It was brought over from England in the 1700's to satisfy the need for hunting on the east coast. The gray fox, it seemed, would not oblige hunters by running away when chased—it simply went into a burrow or up a tree. The red fox was also relocated throughout the United States in support of the burgeoning fur industry.

The gray fox is nocturnal and crepuscular—active at dawn or dusk—which makes it difficult to spot. It beds down during most of the day. If you see a fox, it is more likely of the red variety. I have seen more than one red fox in broad daylight around the developed area of the local airport. I have even had them in my backyard.

Weighing between seven and fifteen pounds, the gray fox can reach fourteen to fifteen inches in height. It can be up to 44" long, with a 17" tail. It is grizzled gray above and reddish on its lower sides, chest, and back of its head. Because of this reddish coloration, it is often confused with the red fox. However, the red variety lacks any gray coloration: it is entirely red, with white patches at the throat, chest, and tip of its tail. The red fox is also slightly larger than the gray.

Mating between January and April, a litter of three or four kits is born between March and May. Birth occurs in a den, which they either excavate themselves or establish in a natural cavity such as a rock overhang or cave. They can also make a den underneath a building. The den is seldom used after the mating season.

The gray eats a variety of foods, but mostly subsists on the cottontail rabbit. It also feeds on birds, as well as small mammals such as mice and voles. Insects, such as grasshoppers and crickets, are also an important staple. Plant foods include corn, persimmons, pokeweed fruit, nuts, berries, and grasses. It will cache larger amounts of food, covering it with dirt or moss.

Man has long been the most significant enemy of the gray fox. Often declaring all-out war, they are shot, trapped, poisoned, and run over. Absent man, it has no real enemies, though bobcats, where abundant, may kill some, and domestic dogs may take a few. But this predator, ever sly as the adage goes, remains near the top of the food chain.

Source:
Whitaker, John O. *Mammals of Indiana*, Indiana University Press, 1996

Dance of the Red-Tailed Hawk

Anyone who has ever stopped to watch a hawk in flight will know that this is one of the natural world's most elegant phenomena.

— John Burnside

The spring mating ritual of the red-tailed hawk (*Buteo jamaicensis*) is poetry in flight. I can pause for long moments and watch their beautiful display until these wonderful birds soar from view. For a moment, I am carried away with them in this dance of new life, thankful for spring and the gift of rebirth that has been with us for millennia.

In a chapter of my life now past, I worked near the local airport and enjoyed watching a red-tailed hawk as it hunted in the vacant fields outside my office window—so much so that I never wanted to see this slice of urban wild developed. The hawk often perched on a light stanchion, which gave it a good view of the open fields and the voles that inhabited the grassy stubble. Suddenly taking flight, it would pounce on its prey. I knew that all did not end well for the vole, but it was simply the reality of nature and its cycle of birth and death.

When they are on or near the ground, I am always in awe of the size of this hawk. They can reach up to twenty-two inches long and have a wingspan of up to fifty-six inches. Their wingspan is just a foot shorter than I am tall. Their sharp bill, used for tearing apart their prey, can be over an inch long in the adult and has a frightening, downward turn at the end. Sharp talons, the hooked claws on all birds of prey, help insure that their meal won't escape. If I were prey, none of these things would give me comfort.

The red-tail is our most common *buteo*, a genus of large, wide-winged, short-tailed soaring hawks. Its territory includes the entire continental U.S., Canada, Alaska, and Mexico, with Indiana being well within its year-around range. Color variations exist across its territory, but the most common diagnostic marking is the rufous or red tail of the adults. Their prey includes voles, mice, birds, snakes and insects, but they will take larger mammals such as rabbits and squirrels. Although some forty years ago, I still remember seeing a red-tail take a pigeon on the roof of a downtown building. The hapless bird was quickly dispatched and then carried to a nearby tree. The moment, clearly etched in my mind, was the first time I had such a close vantage point to a hawk's kill: a primordial feeling came over me.

No matter when or where I see them, I am always in awe of these powerful raptors. Maybe they are being harassed by smaller birds, feathered fighter pilots attempting to chase the enemy from the field. I am never quite sure who I want to win the battle, but the hawk usually retreats rather than put up a fight. I may see this beautiful bird sitting on a post, closely observing an open field, keeping an eye out for its next meal. I always listen for that wheezy *keeeeer* in the spring, hopeful that I will once again witness poetry in the sky.

> The spotted hawk swoops by and accuses me, he
> complains of my gab and my loitering.
> I too am not a bit tamed, I too am untranslatable,
> I sound my barbaric yawp over the roofs of the world.
> The last scud of day holds back for me,
> It flings my likeness after the rest and true as any on the
> shadow'd wilds,
> It coaxes me to the vapor and the dusk.

Walt Whitman, Song of Myself, verse 52

Source:
Clark, William S. & Brian K. Wheeler. *Hawks of North America*. Peterson Field Guides, Houghton and Mifflin, 2001.

Whitman, Walt. *Leaves of Grass*, Canterbury Classics, 2015.

V. HOME GROUND

After the Leaves Fall

How many flutterings before they rest quietly in their graves! They that soared so loftily, how contentedly they return to dust again, and are laid low, resigned to lie and decay at the foot of the tree, and afford nourishment to new generations of their kind, as well as to flutter on high! They teach us how to die. One wonders if the time will ever come when men, with their boasted faith in immortality, will lie down as gracefully and as ripe.

- Henry David Thoreau, *Autumnal Tints*

Late fall and winter are the seasons of browns and grays. The fall colors are gone; the leaves, having floated gracefully to the ground, return to the soil. The winter solstice is just around the corner and with it will come the shortest period of daylight and the longest night of the year. Many resign themselves to that long slog to spring.

Perhaps we tend to spend more of our days indoors, eagerly awaiting that first spring flower. Our trips outside might be a quick walk from our car to the store, home or office. For me, it is a great time to be outdoors and discover the sights and sounds of the new season. Just as much of nature has fallen asleep, so much more comes alive during the winter months.

On an early morning hike in Brown County, I experienced the sights and sounds of the winter landscape. I heard the rattle of the dry leaves of the pin oaks and beech trees in the early morning wind. The pine trees hummed their beautiful melody as the wind passed through their needles. I saw the greens of the cedar trees against the brown landscape. I discovered a turkey feather, its dark brown and white hash marks contrasted against a soft bed of pine needles. I heard sleet striking the dried leaves on the woodland floor. Traces of animals that call the woods home were exposed on the ground: the chipmunk's excavations, a ground hog's burrow, a snake skin, and the nest of a field mouse. The skeletons of the goldenrod, winter sentinels, stood guard in a woodland meadow.

The leaves that once hid the intricate patterns of branches were gone, exposing the unique shape of each tree. The bird and squirrel nests, built to nurture last season's young, were now exposed. Clouds hurtled through the sky and leaves tumbled along the ground, pushed by a brisk fall wind. Picking up a sugar maple leaf, I was reminded of more than just the winter months that lay ahead. I felt the spring sun, the nurturing rain, and saw the bright colors that will come once again and paint the land.

There will certainly be dark, cold, snowy days ahead. Before spring awakens, let's brave the elements and take the time to explore our wonderful winter world. There is so much waiting to be discovered.

When the leaves fall, the whole earth is a cemetery pleasant to walk in. I love to wander and muse over them in their graves. Here are no lying or vain epitaphs.

- Henry David Thoreau, *Autumnal Tints*

Land of Ice

Wooly mammoths, reindeer and musk ox once roamed the landscape. Ice towered high above the tallest trees. Indiana in winter, yes, but obviously not last winter. The Pleistocene Epoch and continental glaciation were periods millions of years ago when glaciers advanced into North America and covered a significant part of the landscape. The glaciers that found their way into Indiana originated from the Laurentide ice sheet, which was centered in the Hudson Bay area. A similar glacial period also occurred simultaneously in Eurasia.

Beginning almost three million years ago, the Nebraskan glacial period began in North America. It was followed by three more glacial periods: the Kansan, Illinoian, and finally the Wisconsinan. Each of these glacial periods was separated by one or more interglacial or warming periods.

There is limited evidence that Indiana was directly impacted by the Nebraskan glacial period and limited knowledge of Kansan glaciation in Indiana. Most obvious is the impact of the Illinoisan and Wisconsinan glacial periods. Much of the contemporary landscape in Indiana is a direct result of these two glacial periods. However, not all of Indiana was glaciated during these two periods. A significant part of southern Indiana was left untouched by glacial ice and this hilly terrain provides a stark contrast to the flatter, glaciated areas of Indiana.

If you were in downtown Columbus, Indiana during the Illinoian, you would have been covered by ice. During the Wisconsinan period, you would have been standing against a wall of ice over a mile high. The depth of the Laurentide ice sheet at its origin in the Hudson Bay area was estimated to be at least 10,000 feet.

Residents of Columbus might notice a pond on the right side of the road as they travel north on Taylor Road. Just past 31st Street is a fine example of a kettle pond. It was created when a large chunk of ice calved off the glacier and depressed the ground, thereby creating this glacial remnant. Many have mistaken it for a retention pond like the one a few blocks farther north.

Ice of this significance had an impact on Indiana's terrain. Whether it is glacial outwash, sand dunes, the natural lakes of northern Indiana, glacial erratics, moraines, or other glacial features, we live in a land impacted by ice.

> *To say that for destruction ice*
> *Is also great*
> *And would suffice."*

— from *"Fire and Ice"* by Robert Frost

Sources:

Wayne, William J., Ed. *Natural Features of Indiana,* Indiana Academy of Science, 1966

Jackson, Marion T. *The Natural History of Indiana,* Indiana University Press, 1997

Frost, Robert. *The Poetry of Robert Frost.* Holt, Rinehart, and Winston, 1969

The Garden

At the moment, we are in the midst of a winter storm that likely will dump about five or six inches of snow locally—so this may seem like an odd time to write about gardening. I walked outside earlier today and the only thing that remains of my garden are the skeletons of the wildflowers from last season. My thoughts were soon propelled towards spring with the arrival of the season's first garden seed catalog in the mail.

Gardening has been part of my life since I was six or seven. It began with my grandfather's tomato and rhubarb plants in his backyard on Cherry Street in Columbus, Indiana, punctuated with trips to my uncle's farm near Waymansville to pick up a basket of cow manure every growing season. That always made for a rather stinky ride back into town, but boy, did it work wonders on those tomatoes. I remember tilling up my own spot in our backyard on Chestnut Street when I was twelve; I fondly recall the stand of popcorn I grew. Gardening got into my blood at an early age—or maybe it was simply regenerated from my ancestral, agrarian roots. My parents' garden was a bit more substantial, with long rows of green beans for canning and cucmbers for pickling. There were more than enough tomatoes and sweet corn for neighbors and friends.

Although I have never had the garden that my parents once had, I have enjoyed a garden in every season that I have had my own home. I cannot imagine a spring where I would not be digging in the soil, patiently putting seeds and plants in the ground. To not smell the perfume of fresh soil, herbs, and garden plants, to not feel the seeds of the future in the palm of my hand, would be to give up a bit of my spirit's connection to the earth.

Gardening is one outward manifestation of my connection to nature. Whether holding a fresh tomato in my hand or admiring an ox-eye daisy growing in my wildflower garden, each reminds me of the presence of the divine in those natural wonders that I hold so dear. There is something refreshing about washing away the cares of the day outdoors among my vegetables, herbs, and blooming perennials: a touch of nature as close as my backyard. So, until spring arrives, I will keep the garden catalogs close at hand in hopeful anticipation.

If you have a garden and a library, you have everything you need.

- Cicero from Varro, in *Ad Familiares* IX, 4

Downstream

Often, I think about how the waters of the East Fork of the White River, flowing through my hometown of Columbus, Indiana, are connected to the whole world. Suddenly, places such as Rio de Janeiro, Shanghai, Alexandria, Portsmouth, LeHavre, or Sydney don't seem that far away.

This realization came to me in grade school when I saw the short movie, *Paddle to the Sea*, based on Holling C. Holling's book by the same name. A young boy in the Nipigong country north of Lake Superior carves a small wooden canoe and releases it in a nearby creek. The movie follows its travels through the Great Lakes and into the St. Lawrence River, where it eventually ends up in the hands of a lighthouse keeper on the coast of Newfoundland.

The East Fork is formed at Mill Race Park in Columbus at the confluence of the Driftwood and Flat Rock rivers. One of the most significant river systems in southern Indiana, it meanders south and west. It passes by small, rural communities such as Sparksville, Ft. Ritner, Buddha, Williams, and Shoals. It flows by natural features such as Jug Rock, Old Man's Nose, Hindostan Falls, and Devil's Elbow. Countless rivers, streams, and creeks feed into the river along the way, draining thousands of square miles of the Hoosier state before the river meets with the

West Fork northeast of Petersburg in Gibson County. Now the White River, it eventually joins the Wabash across from Mt. Carmel, Illinois.

We are not isolated from the local, regional or global impact of our activities just because the waters of the East Fork—or any river—leave our sights. What we put on our yards, down our drains, on our agricultural lands, or what comes out of our industrial and municipal facilities cannot simply be shrugged off. We don't even have to live near a river to have an impact. Water is life, and disregard for its health is detrimental to present and future generations. Whether the waters of the East Fork are flowing past Buddha or Devil's Elbow, or lapping a distant shore, the river carries our legacy. We must remain mindful of this and work hard to leave our neighbors downstream a healthy river to enjoy.

Source: Indiana Atlas & Gazetteer, Delorme, 1998

Have Faith

Spring - an experience in immortality.

- Henry David Thoreau

Spring is still a way off, with March 20th marking the vernal equinox, the day when the sun will shine directly on the equator and the length of day and night will be nearly equal. If you buy into the groundhog's predictions, we still have six more weeks of winter in these parts. My *Old Farmer's Almanac* predicts that mid-March will be among the snowiest periods in the Ohio Valley. (Gosh, it even says that there might be snow the first week of April. Whatever happened to April showers? Don't put your snow shovels away too soon).

If you are at all like me, you are getting a little anxious to forget the winter, which has seemed a bit colder and drearier this season. Does it sometimes feel like nature is asleep, or maybe has abandoned us entirely? The trees are barren and, when the snow is gone, browns and grays dominate the landscape. There doesn't appear to be a whole lot moving out there when we glance out the window. But is it really asleep? Did nature turn over only to finally be awakened in a few months when the sun warms the soil and the day lasts a little longer? Be assured we have not been abandoned to a new Ice Age—at least not yet. The signs of life are around us.

The birds that visit my feeders remind me that life goes on. Some of their comrades went south, just as some of mine did. But a number of birds have remained. The familiar cardinal, the junco, a variety of woodpeckers, the blue jay, the house finch, and many others have called my backyard home this winter. The male and female cardinals against the white snow have made for a beautiful contrast in colors.

Maybe we have caught a glimpse of some of our four-legged residents, too. The ever-present fox squirrels have raided my feeders all winter. A hike in the Brown County woods revealed a whitetail deer, startled from its hiding place. There were raccoon tracks along the creek bank and a flock of turkeys moved through the woods, scratching their own trail in the snow. The morning hoot of a barred owl—*who-who-who-cooks-for-you*—reminded me of busy mice and chipmunks—fine meals—along the woodland floor. Coyote tracks provide more evidence that the woods are still alive and teeming with activity, even when we have abandoned them for the warmth of our hearths.

Take heart, for below your feet and above your head spring awaits, as it has for eons. The trees will soon bud, the spring wildflowers will emerge, the days and nights will be warmer, and the birds of summer will return. The bright sun will warm your soul and the fragrance of spring will help you shed the memories of the winter. I, too, long for spring, but this winter hasn't been so bad when I think of all the life out there, even on the bleakest of days.

They were pleasant spring days, in which the winter of man's discontent was thawing as well as the earth, and the life that had lain torpid began to stretch itself.

- Henry David Thoreau, *Walden*

A Woodland Stream

Time is but the stream I go a-fishing in. I drink at it; but while I drink I see the sandy bottom and detect how shallow it is. Its thin current slides away, but eternity remains.

– Henry David Thoreau, *Walden*

A walk in the woods is a journey of discovery, both of self and the natural world. Often, I pause to take in the moment, explore its meaning and listen to its song. Perhaps it is the wind blowing through a stand of pines, the soft babble of a small woodland stream, the rain falling on the leaves lying on the woodland floor, the birds flitting through the branches of the trees, the hoot of a barred owl, or the howl of a distant coyote. Each experience in the woods builds upon the last and strengthens the inseparable bond I have with nature.

You can follow a woodland stream uphill in Brown County State Park until you reach the point it emerges from the underlying rock. It is there that the soft trickle of water begins its long journey to the sea. But, it isn't the thought of those distant shores that occupies me: it is just this small stream descending through these woods, its soft currents gliding gently over the 250 million-year-old Mississippian Age sandstones. This stream has more allure than a river cascading through the granite of some distant mountain range. This is my home ground, the place where my boot soles have collected the most dirt, where my experiences always create a flood of memories, where my flesh and bones belong.

In late fall and early winter, the character of this small woodland stream lies hidden from view, bone dry and buried under a blanket of leaves. It isn't until the ground freezes and snowmelt and rain begin to push the leaves downstream that its hidden beauty will be revealed. The work of ages soon becomes apparent: stones of different shapes and sizes fill the streambed with a variety of colors, each created over millions of years by the interaction of the sandstone with water and minerals. The reds, browns, and tans of these stones create an endless canvas of color, each square foot, each yard as unique as a fingerprint, a ribbon of color wandering through the woods. The crystal-clear water flowing over the bedrock shelves creates small cascades, adding to the beauty of the woods.

It is humbling to pick up a stone from the stream, hold it in my hand and gaze upon millions of years of the earth's history. At the same time, I gaze upon the buds on the trees, the wildflowers waiting to bloom, all the new growth that spring will soon bring to the woods—reminders of new life, of new possibilities. I also think of the stone and each single grain of sand within it and the ripples that fade away after I drop it into the stream. In the end, I am like a grain of sand, a small ripple in time, disappearing into eternity. Before I fade away, will I look back and know that I dove deeply into life's stream, swam down to its depths, and explored its deepest currents? Or, when I finally wash up on some distant shore, will I have left these things unexplored? Will I have left the stones in my stream unturned?

Source:
Geologic Story of Brown County State Park, State of Indiana, Department of Natural Resources. State Park Guide 9, 1981.

Today's Weather

Widespread Heavy to Excessive Rainfall Event in the Lower/Middle Mississippi Valley into the Ohio Valley

Slow-moving Tropical Depression Gordon continues to bring heavy to excessive rains across portions of the lower Mississippi Valley. Friday, moisture from Gordon will spread north into the Middle Mississippi Valley and interact with an existing frontal boundary, where several days of rain has already saturated the soils, increasing the potential for excessive rain and flash floods.

National Weather Service,
September 7, 2018

S
o said the National Weather Service last Friday, and they weren't wrong. It has rained steadily since before dawn on Saturday and has continued into today, leaving us with 3.7 inches according to my backyard rain

gauge. Seems to me like an appropriate time to talk about the weather.

Frank McKinney "Kin" Hubbard was a Hoosier cartoonist, humorist, and journalist. He was the creator of the cartoon *Abe Martin of Brown County*, which ran in U.S. newspapers from 1904 until his death in 1930. He was the originator of many quips. One of my favorites is, "Don't knock th' weather. Nine-tenths o' th' people couldn' start a conversation if it didn' change once in a while."

Regardless of 'whether' it dominates my conversation, weather does occupy my daily affairs. I think about it when I get up in the morning and when I go to bed at night. I think about how cold or hot it will be, and what the prevailing winds will bring to the day. It tells me what to wear, whether I can do any gardening, whether a hike in the woods will be washed out, or whether I should get the snow shovel out of the shed.

Sometimes, I get caught in the weather doldrums and each day bleeds into the next. Another hot day, another day of rain, more cold, "expect a high of this and low of that", "the relative humidity will be this" or "the barometer is rising". Our daily newspaper devotes a half page to local and national weather statistics. I can find the high and low temperatures yesterday in Des Moines and the river stages of the East Fork of the White River at Columbus and Seymour. Heck, I can even find out when the moon rises and sets.

It can be easy for me to get lost in the statistics sometimes and lose sight that weather is also personal; it transcends mere statistics and takes me into a more spiritual realm. There is something deep inside me that is stirred by a thunderstorm in the middle of the night, the lightning illuminating the room like midday; or, by walking in the woods during a snowstorm as the wind stirs the tree branches and the snow pelts my face; also, the first hard frost of the season, glistening in the morning sun; the dew on the grass in summer, like pearls on the ground; or the character of each cumulus cloud, floating above me in the autumn sky.

I love the change that each season brings. It is the weather more than anything that will propel me into a pensive mood. Watching a thunderstorm roll in from the west reminds me of the awesome power of nature: the cool wind charging ahead of the storm strikes my face; the leaves turn over in the trees, the thunder rolls and the lightning flashes...and then, the first raindrop. I refuse to go inside until the rational part of my brain suggests it would be best.

The weather touches each of us, whether consciously or not. Some may treat it casually, until it blows a tree down in their front yard. I come from a long line of farmers, carpenters, and preachers—the latter profession perhaps watching a little more closely for thunder and lightning. Mom's grandparents came to this country from Germany. One was an accomplished orchardman, herbalist, and farmer and the other a landholder and well-respected farmer in southern Bartholomew County. My maternal grandfather farmed and managed the local feed store.

The Illinois Irish, on my paternal side, were a bit more colorful and with just a hint of scandal thrown in. My great-grandfather, born out of wedlock, was fathered by the local schoolmaster. My grandfather was a carpenter and worked for a dollar an hour in the 1930s. I have always enjoyed John Prine's song, "Grandpa was a Carpenter", but mine didn't chain-smoke Camel straights—he preferred Chesterfields. Another great-grandfather was a

Southern Baptist preacher, preaching fire and brimstone from the pulpit, and the other delivered the mail by horse and buggy, gently prodding his horse along, whatever the weather.

Whether hammering a nail, planting corn, delivering the mail, or haranguing the congregation from the pulpit, I'm sure they all payed close attention to the weather. The weather plays a bit less of a role in my work, as I am able to write these words in the comfort of my study, even as the rain continues to fall outside. Like my ancestors, though, I will always be aware of the weather, whether as a point of conversation, a reminder of the beauty and power that comes from the skies, or as a stimulus for much deeper thought.

The BLT (aka, the Bacon, Lettuce, and Tomato Sandwich)

The seeds of my BLT were planted in the dead of winter when the first garden catalogs arrived in my mailbox. I glanced through the pages and the explosion of color—notably absent during the winter months—jumped from the pages: tomatoes in a multitude of varieties and hues, with names like Red Lightning, Mr. Stripey, Little Mama, Green Zebra, Big Zac, Cherokee Purple, and Oh Happy Day.

I love tomatoes about any way you can fix them: raw, roasted, fried green, in a tart, stuffed, or pickled. But there is one way I enjoy a tomato that defines summer for me, and that is in a BLT. Of all the things I plant in my garden, my tomatoes define it. The lettuce can go to seed, the zucchini can rot on the vine, and the beetles can chew up my kale, but my tomato plants are my children, my offspring.

My BLT began to take shape last fall. I prepared my garden soil by adding the summer's compost and then heaping on a good pile of late autumn leaves. The rotting jack-o-lanterns from Halloween were thrown in for good measure. Perhaps to my neighbor's dismay, I liberally threw kitchen waste on top of the pile throughout the winter months: egg shells, coffee grounds, and vegetable peelings.

As the days grew longer and the first of May approached, I began to get the itch to hit the nursery and find out what varieties of tomatoes would be available this season. I always choose carefully, never wanting a plant that has already fruited or contains too many flowers. Preferring a plant about 8 to 10 inches tall, I want the energy it gives to bearing fruit to come from my garden soil—no artificial ingredients of any kind, purely organic.

Although I usually plant what I call a standard bearer such as Early Girl, Better Boy, or Beefsteak, I always choose an heirloom variety to spice up the kitchen a bit. This year, I chose a Black Prince, native to Siberia. I must admit that it was hard to imagine a tomato growing on the tundra. It has done just fine in my backyard.

As I do with all my plants, I nurtured each one carefully, giving it just the right amount of water and watching closely for pests. My efforts soon bore fruit, and I plucked the first tomato from the vine just over a week ago. Tempting as it might have been to carve up the first harvest into a few raw slices and consume it *au naturel*, I instead sliced it thin in anticipation of that first BLT.

The BLT, the consummate summer sandwich, a staple of my diet since childhood—a sandwich of the vine and turf: two slices of whole wheat bread, toasted to perfection; mayonnaise spread liberally and evenly on each slice. Then, carefully picked lettuce leaves from the garden form the second layer of this specimen of culinary architecture. Atop the crisp, green bed I nestle the fruit of the vine, quarter inch slices from a perfectly ripe, blemish-free tomato. Finally, I add the bacon: thick-cut and fried just short of crispy. After placing the last slice of bread on top,

I survey my masterpiece for a moment before I take the first bite: my mouth comes alive and I savor each bite that follows, wishing that my stomach was just a little larger and that another BLT lay in wait.

The taste of this delightful sandwich conjures up memories of summers past: the *whirr* of locusts, sparklers on the 4th of July, corn on the cob, watermelon and cantaloupe fresh from the market, baseball games, fishing with a cane pole and bobber, going barefoot in the grass—all part of my Midwestern experience. I still have my childhood copy of Alice Low's book, *Summer*, and it still resonates with me. I particularly enjoy her closing sentence:

> "We stay awake and think of things...the
> happy things that summer brings!"

I vividly remember crawling into bed at the end of a glorious summer day, tired but fulfilled, wondering as I drifted off what adventures the next day would bring. If I continue to choose the seeds of my garden wisely, if I plant and cultivate them properly, I can again savor that first BLT and all the memories that come with it. Spring planting and summer fruit drive away the melancholy of winter.

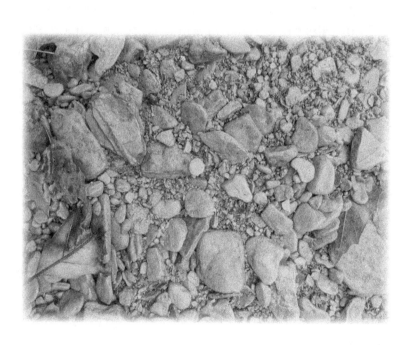

My Study

After I've gone to my home in the sky, I can imagine my children having a conversation about what to do with my stuff—and I have a LOT of stuff. It would go something like this:

> *Damn, Dad collected a lot of shit, didn't he?*
> *Yeah, what do we do with all these rocks?*
> *Do you want any?*
> *What the hell would I do with a buncha rocks?*
> *Look at all his books! My God, we don't have any room in our house for these.*
> *It's like a freakin library!*
> *Should we have a sale or maybe just bury it all with him?*
> *We'd need a big damn hole in the ground, that's for sure.*
> *He's probably up there laughin' at us right now.*
> *Yeah, I reckon it's payback for all the crap we left him to clean up when we were kids.*

I just finished reading *On Writing, A Memoir of the Craft,* by Stephen King. My wife enjoys his work, but

I'm really not much into fiction. I think Kurt Vonnegut's *Hocus Pocus* was the last novel I read, and that was over sixteen years ago. In *On Writing*, King writes about finding the right place to write, a space you can call your own. For me, that space is my study, my corner of our little Cape Cod on Roselawn Avenue. There is no question that my fingerprints are all over this space.

When I am in the woods, I explore ideas, plumb the depths so to speak, but it is when I sit down in my study that these ideas come to life, when my brain and fingers connect. There is a little bit of everything in my study. Around me are hundreds of pieces I have collected over the years. Some might look at it and say, "What a mess!" I prefer to call it "detritus"—and it's *my* detritus, dammit! I can take a piece in my hand and recall the particulars of its origin. Whether rock, knife, fossil, artwork, knick-knack, or whatever, each one is a piece of my lifetime.

I thought it would be fun to put together a short list that would provide a glimpse into my study and perhaps, into me. As I compiled the list, a wave of memories flooded over me, fifty to be exact, and a tsunami of my life's experiences:

1. Thirty-Four volumes of personal journals (I'm working on Thirty-Five—I prefer the *Moleskine Classic Notebook* with ruled pages)
2. My grandfather's Case pocketknife
3. A Black Widow spider preserved in alcohol
4. An oak gall
5. A snakeskin
6. A snake skeleton
7. My grandfather's cane fishing pole
8. A barometer

9. A U.S. Military Engineer's compass from 1918
10. A picture of my grandmother and aunt, circa 1910
11. My 3rd grade picture
12. My baby shoes, bronzed (Thank you, Mom.)
13. The skull of a raccoon
14. A jar of Ohio buckeyes
15. A polished Petoskey stone
16. A variety of pine cones
17. A variety of art pieces created by my daughters
18. Pictures of my wife and children
19. An old pair of wood snowshoes
20. Two kaleidoscopes (sometimes I need to see the world a little differently)
21. Ironwood carving of a bull moose
22. A ghost made by my daughter, Katie, using Kleenex, a rubber band, and a Sharpie
23. A picture of my oldest and best friend, Horace (RIP)
24. Green Bay Packers and St. Louis Cardinals memorabilia
25. My mom's early needlepoint work depicting a cottage in the woods
26. A brachiopod fossil
27. A vase of dried oak leaves and weeds
28. A microscope
29. Books, books, and more books
30. My Eagle Scout medal (1976)
31. A Green Darner Dragonfly
32. A turkey call
33. Geodes
34. A painted rock that says, "My Dad Rocks" from Sarah

35. The broken tip of a graphite fishing rod (a very long story)
36. A Taylor wet-dry bulb hygrometer
37. Prayer beads
38. My mother's Kodak Pony camera
39. A whitetail deer skull and antlers
40. Sand from Oval Beach in Saugatuck, Michigan
41. Buddhist prayer flags
42. A picture of Mom and Dad
43. A LOT of rocks
44. A King Edward cigar box that belonged to my grandfather
45. A rattlesnake's rattle
46. A Barlow pocketknife
47. An Indian arrowhead
48. A Trilobite fossil
49. The jawbone of a squirrel
50. The small, green plastic rat I had in my pocket the day I was fired

On the wall above my desk, a small wooden box frames a quote from one of Thoreau's letters. It reads, "I am grateful for what I am and have. My thanksgiving is perpetual." He goes on to add, "It is surprising how contented one can be with nothing definite, only a sense of existence." I am perpetually grateful for my existence and the enjoyment I get from sitting in my corner, writing these words. I'm also sure I will be adding to the detritus of my life: more "stuff" for my kids to clean up when I'm gone.

Fooled Again

Every time I think I might have her figured out, nature reminds me that I am on a fool's errand. She consistently humbles, and every once in a while makes me look like a doggone idiot. I would rather live in her world, though, than in some man-made, gadget-centric one. I would truly be a fool if I stayed in the house all day, tethered to some electronic gadget, or thought that sixty hours a week in some office would be a good use of my time.

I remember quite a few times when nature played me for a fool. This usually happened when I became a bit too cocky, a bit overconfident in my skills as an outdoorsman. Experiences like being chased into the undergrowth by a cow moose, dive-bombed by a great horned owl, attacked by a blue jay, or receiving multiple bee stings have all served to bring me down a few notches.

Just this morning, I was hiking in Brown County State Park and stepped on a moss-covered rock hidden under the leaves. My feet went flying out from under me and down I went, butt first. As I got up, I pondered an age-old question: If a man takes a tumble alone in a forest, does anyone hear his cry of embarrassment? I sheepishly looked around to see if anyone had seen me.

While in Ohio visiting family for the holidays, a few of

my fellow revelers decided to walk off the afternoon meal. Enjoying the uncharacteristic warmth of a late December day, we wandered over to the neighbor's pond.

Rounding the corner of their house, I spied a great blue heron at pond's edge. Quickly, I prepared my camera for what I was sure would be among the best photographs ever taken of this bird. Shooting rapid fire, I stealthily approached the heron, waving the enthralled group back, lest they startle my subject.

I marveled at how still the heron was, wondering whether it was in search of prey or just deep in thought. I crept ever closer while my two daughters followed behind me, engaged in chatter. I shushed them like a librarian. Moving closer to the bird, I began to see the outline of each feather, amazed that it hadn't taken flight.

At about twenty feet away, I began to wonder whether I might pose with it, get a selfie or two. Then, I realized my error: I was stalking a decoy. Uproarious laughter broke out among my friends as they also realized we'd been had.

Some thirty photographs of this "bird" remain on my hard drive. I have kept them as a reminder that nature can even use a little man-made material to play me for a fool.

Acknowledgments

Writing my first book has been an adventure into the unknown, an exploration of my deeper self. I am grateful for my late mother and father, who provided those epic summer vacations and who always encouraged me to explore and never dashed my hopes. Also, for my maternal grandfather, Alf Borgman, and all those trips to the country and Saturday afternoon baseball games on TV; my Uncle Frank and Aunt Myrtle Borgman, who always welcomed me to their farm and allowed me to go exploring; my best friend, the late Horace Ballard, whose friendship was unconditional; my former scoutmaster, the late Don McFarland, simply the best Scoutmaster an Eagle Scout could have hoped for; and my Friday hiking partner, Marc Vance and those shots of Maker's Mark to cap off our morning adventures. Finally, for my brother and sisters: they have each been so good to me. Family is powerful!

The following people and things, past and present, have also contributed in the spiritual crafting of this work. They each have helped me open my eyes to the world. I thank Henry David Thoreau, Sigurd Olson, Ralph Waldo Emerson, Edwin Way Teale, Wang Wei, Robert Frost, Walt Whitman, Loren Eisley, Rachel Carson, David Budbill, Aldo Leopold, Hsieh Ling-yun, George

Page and the PBS series Nature, Yuan Mei, Baudelier, Thomas Merton, Annie Dillard, Roger Tory Peterson, Li Bai, Rimbaud, Wendell Berry, Du Fu, John Muir, Lao-Tzu, Jesse Stuart, Matsuo Basho, Jesus Christ, Buddha, Vishnu, Rumi, Ann Zwinger, Chuang-Tzu, my ancestors, the Great Lakes, Brown County State Park, Boy Scouts, Isle Royale National Park, Mother Nature, and my home ground.

I am especially indebted to my editor, Krista Hill. Thank you for doing a great job keeping me on point. Your editorial touch has been wonderful. Also, to Heather for helping format my pictures; I knew there was a reason I hired you all those years ago. Finally, to Lucinda; thanks for listening to me all these years.

But, I simply couldn't have gotten this far without my wife, Tracy. She is my cheerleader, encouraging me when my self-doubt puts me in a funk. Also, a thank you and my abiding love for each of my children, Charlie, Sam, Katie, and Sarah. I write for all of you.

Thank you, one and all. I will toast those no longer with us with a little Kentucky bourbon; meanwhile, those of you still present in my world are welcome to stop by some-time for a drink and some finding of common ground.

No human things
Guitar or flute

Quite match up
To nature's music

Du Fu from *The Cricket,* 759 AD

Suggested Reading

There are a number of books that have added color to my outlook on life and nature. Here are just a few...

Allen, Durward L. *The Wolves of Minong – Their Vital Role in a Wild Community.* Houghton Mifflin Company, 1979.

Bashō, Matsuo. *Narrow Road to the Interior and Other Writings.* Translated by Sam Hamil, Shambala Classics, 1998.

Berry, Wendell. *Life is a Miracle.* Counterpoint, 2001.

Berry, Wendell. *Another Turn of the Crank.* Counterpoint, 1995.

Boy Scouts of America. *Fieldbook for Boys and Men.* Boy Scouts of America, 1971.

Boy Scouts of America. *Boy Scout Handbook,* Boy Scouts of America, 1965.

Brady, Bernard and Mark Neuzil. *A Spiritual Field Guide.* Brazos Press, 2005.

Brown, Vinson. *The Amateur Naturalist's Handbook.* Prentice Hall Press, 1980.

Budbill, David. *Moment to Moment.* Copper Canyon Press, 1999.

Budbill, David. *While We've Still Got Feet.* Copper Canyon Press, 2005.

Byrd, Admiral Richard E. *Alone*. Kodansha International, 1995.

Chuang Tzu. *The Inner Chapters*. Translated by David Hinton, Counterpoint, 1997.

Dillard, Annie. *Pilgrim at Tinker Creek*. Harper's Magazine Press, 1974.

Eisley, Loren. *The Immense Journey*. Vintage Books, 1959

Emerson, Ralph Waldo. Self-Reliance. *The Annotated Emerson*, edited by David Mikics, The Belknap Press, 2012, Pages 160-185.

Herzog, Maurice. *Annapurna*. Lyons Press, 2010.

Hornbein, Thomas F. *Everst – West Ridge*. The Mountaineers, 2002.

King, Stephen E. *On Writing – A Memoir of the Craft*. Scribner, 2010.

Lathem, Edward Connery, editor. *The Poetry of Robert Frost*. Holt, Rinehart, and Winston, 1975.

Leopold, Aldo. *A Sand County Almanac*. Oxford University Press, 1968.

Lao-Tzu. *Tao-Te-Ching*. Translated by Red Pine, Copper Canyon Press, 2009.

McPhee, John. *Basin and Range*. Farrar, Straus and Giroux, 1981.

McPhee, John. *In Suspect Terrain*. Farrar, Straus and Giroux, 1988.

McPhee, John. *Rising From the Plains*. Farrar, Straus and Giroux, 1986.

Merton, Thomas. *The Way of Chuang Tzu*. New Directions, 1965.

Merton, Thomas. *When the Trees Say Nothing*. Edited by Kathleen Deignan, Sorin Books, 2008

Muir, John. *Spiritual Writings*. Orbis Books, 2013.

Muir, John. *Nature Writings*. Edited by William Cronon, The Library of America, 1997.

Neihardt, John G. *Black Elk Speaks*. University of Nebraska Press, 1989.

Olson, Sigurd F. *Listening Point*. Alfred A. Knopf, 1974.

Olson, Sigurd F. *Open Horizons*. Alfred A. Knopf, 1969

Olson, Sigurd F. *The Lonely Land*, Alfred A.Knopf, 1961

Olson, Sigurd F. *Reflections from the North Country*. Alfred A. Knopf, 1989.

Peattie, Donald Cutross. *A Natural History of North American Trees*. Trinity University Press, 2013

Peattie, Donald Cutross. *The Road of a Naturalist*. G.K. Hall and Company, 1986.

Peterson, Roger Tory. *A Field Guide to the Birds*. Houghton Mifflin Company, 1947.

Po Chü-I. *The Selected Poems of Po Chü-I*. Translated by David Hinton, A New Directions Book, 1999.

Rumi. *The Essential Rumi*. Translated by Coleman Barks, HarperOne, 2004.

Stonehouse. *The Mountain Poems of Stonehouse*. Translated by Red Pine, Copper Canyon Press, 2014.

Strunk, William Jr. and E.B. White. *The Elements of Style*. Longman, 1999.

Teale, Edwin Way. *Autumn Across America*. St. Martin's Press, 1956.

Teale, Edwin Way. *North with the Spring*. Dodd, Mead, and Company, 1951.

Teale, Edwin Way. *Wandering Through Winter*. Dodd, Mead, and Company, 1965

The Holy Bible, The New International Version, Zondervan, 1991.

Thoreau, Henry David. *Life Without Principle.* Cambridge Edition, Houghton Mifflin Company, 1975, Pages 808-825.

Thoreau, Henry David. *Civil Disobedience.* Cambridge Edition, Houghton Mifflin Company, 1975, Pages 789-808.

Thoreau, Henry David. *Walden.* Houghton Mifflin Company, 1995.

Thoreau, Henry David. *Walking.* Tilbury House Publishers, 2017.

Tu Fu. *The Selected Poems of Tu Fu.* Translated by David Hinton, A New Directions Book, 1989.

Vonnegut, Kurt. *If This Isn't Nice, What Is?* Seven Stories Press, 2016

Vonnegut, Kurt. *Slaughterhouse-Five.* A Laurel Book, 1991.

Wang Wei. *The Selected Poems of Wang Wei.* Translated by David Hinton, A New Directions Book, 2006.

Warriner, John E. *English Composition and Grammar.* Harcourt Brace Jovanovich, 1988.

Whitman, Walt. *Leaves of Grass.* Canterbury Classics, 2012.

Yuan Mei. *I Don't Bow to Buddhas – Selected Poems of Yuan Mei.* Translated by J.P. Seaton, Copper Canyon Press, 1997.

A full list of my field guides can be found at www. uponcommonground.org.

CPSIA information can be obtained
at www.ICGtesting.com
Printed in the USA
LVHW111611050819
626567LV00004B/16/P

9 781480 878044